VEGAN RECIPE BOOK

DELICOUS & PACKED FLAVOUR

JULIA CAMMOILE

Copyright © 2019 by Julia Cammoile

All rights reserved. No part of this book may be used or reproduced by any means, graphic, electronic, or mechanical, including photocopying, recording, taping, or by any information storage retrieval system, without the written permission of the publisher except in the case of brief quotations embodied in critical articles and reviews.

WELCOME!

There are some cool features in this recipe book that will make it easy for you to cook the dishes and also track your food.

TRACKING YOUR FOOD

If you want to keep track of your macronutrients and calories, then all you have to do is scan the barcode on each recipe in your MyFitnessPal™ App and voila.

MEDICAL DISCLAIMER

This recipe book is not designed to replace any advice given to you by a medical practitioner or registered dietician.

All recipes within this book are for information purposes only. If you choose to make a recipe within this book, then you are doing so at your own risk. Please check all the ingredients first to ensure you are not allergic to any of them.

If you think there is any part of the book that might have a negative impact on your health, then please consult a doctor before starting.

Table of Contents

Fruity Protein Oats 1

Raspberry & Pomegranate Chia Seed Pudding.. 3

Fruity Vegan Pancakes 5

Chocolatey Protein Smoothie 7

Beans On Toast 9

Sweet Potato Quesadillas 11

Super Greens Salad 13

Roast Butternut Squash & Spinach Salad 15

Crispy Aubergine Sandwich 17

Chilli, Mango And Black Bean Salad 19

Orzo & Spinach Soup 21

Falafels With Mediterranean Couscous Salad 23

Quinoa & Chickpea Salad 25

Curried Chickpeas On Baked Sweet Potato 27

Lasagne Soup..29

Tofu Stir Fry 31

Sweet Potato & White Bean Chilli..33

Roasted Cauliflower Dhal..35

Vegetable Red Thai Curry 37

Bbq Chickpea & Walnut Burger...39

Chickpea & Red Split Lentil Curry...41

Saag Aloo 43

Red Split Lentil Dahl 45

Vegan Soya Chilli 47

Lentil Pie 49

Butternut Squash Risotto 51

One Pot Chilli Thai Pasta 53

Vegetable Crisps 55

Date Boats 57

Dark Chocolate & Raspberry Muffins 59

FRUITY PROTEIN OATS

(Per Serving) Calories 381 / Carbs 46g / Protein 20g / Fat 13g

Ready in under five minutes, these moreish oats are easy to prepare and ensure that you don't skip breakfast! Adding the blended fruits gives this recipe a lift and finished off this dish perfectly.

Serves 1 Prep Time 4 mins Cook Time 4 mins ## INGREDIENTS 25g (1oz) Strawberries 25g (1oz) Raspberries 25g (1oz) Blueberries 1 tbsp Water 50g (1 3/4oz) Porridge Oats 100ml (1/2cup) Oat Milk 100ml (1/2cup) Water 15g (1/2oz) Banana Vegan Protein Powder (you can use other flavours) A Pinch of Salt 10g (1/4oz) Flaked Almonds	## HOW TO COOK IT Add the first 4 ingredients into a blender and blend until smooth. Once done put to one side. Add the oats, oat milk and water into a saucepan and cook over a medium heat until the mixture thickens. Remove from the heat and add the protein powder and salt, mix well. If the mixture becomes too thick, add a splash of oat milk or water. Add to a bowl and pour the blended fruit mixture over the top and finish with a sprinkle of flaked almonds..

DIETICIAN'S NOTES

Containing a good quantity of protein and slow release carbohydrates, this breakfast should keep you energised throughout the morning. Be sure to choose an oat milk fortified with calcium if you don't consume any dairy.

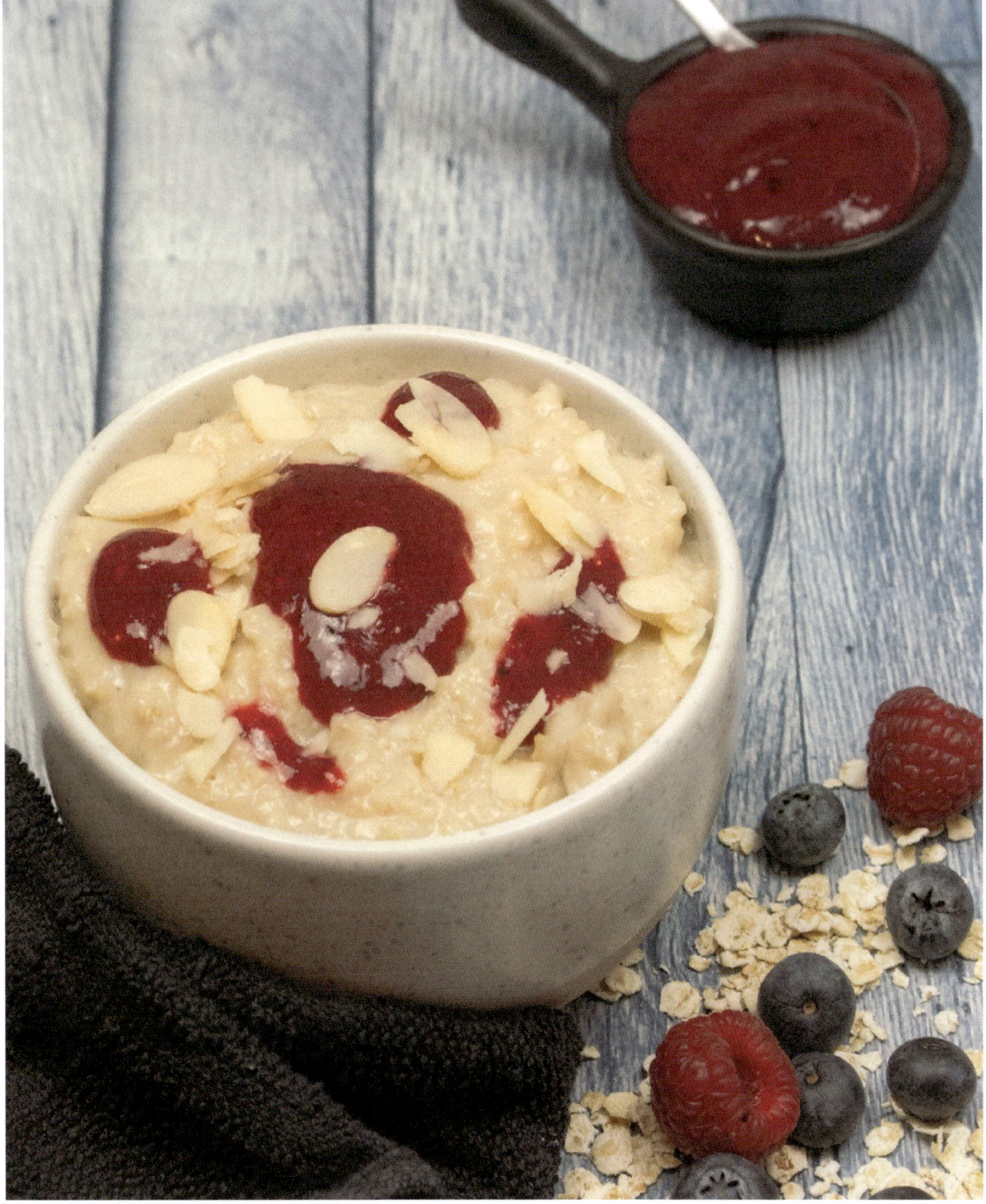

RASPBERRY & POMEGRANATE CHIA SEED PUDDING

(Per Serving) Calories 303 / Carbs 41g / Protein 10g / Fat 11g

(Per Serving) Calories 303 / Carbs 41g / Protein 10g / Fat 11g This fruity chia pudding is perfect for a healthy breakfast or a snack. Pomegranate seeds are packed with antioxidants. Add coconut and cinnamon for extra flavour.

Serves 2 Prep Time 4 mins Fridge Time 20 mins ## INGREDIENTS 4 tbsp Chia Seed ½ tsp Ground Cinnamon Vanilla Extract (a couple of drops) 125ml (½cup) Coconut Milk 60g (2oz) Porridge Oats 80g (2 3/4oz) Raspberries 2 tsp Desiccated Coconut 50g (1 3/4oz) Pomegranate	## HOW TO COOK IT Add the chia seeds, cinnamon, vanilla extract and coconut milk into a mixing bowl. Stir it together and place in the fridge for 20 minutes to set. Once set, remove from the fridge. Add the oats to a glass cup. Then layer the ingredients as follows. Raspberries, chia seed mixtures, desiccated coconut and finish with the pomegranates.

DIETICIAN'S NOTES

Chia seeds and oats are both a great source of fibre. Eating fibre rich foods is a great habit, as high fibre diets have been linked with a lower risk of heart disease, diabetes and bowel cancer. Top with extra fruit to score one of your 5-A-DAY.

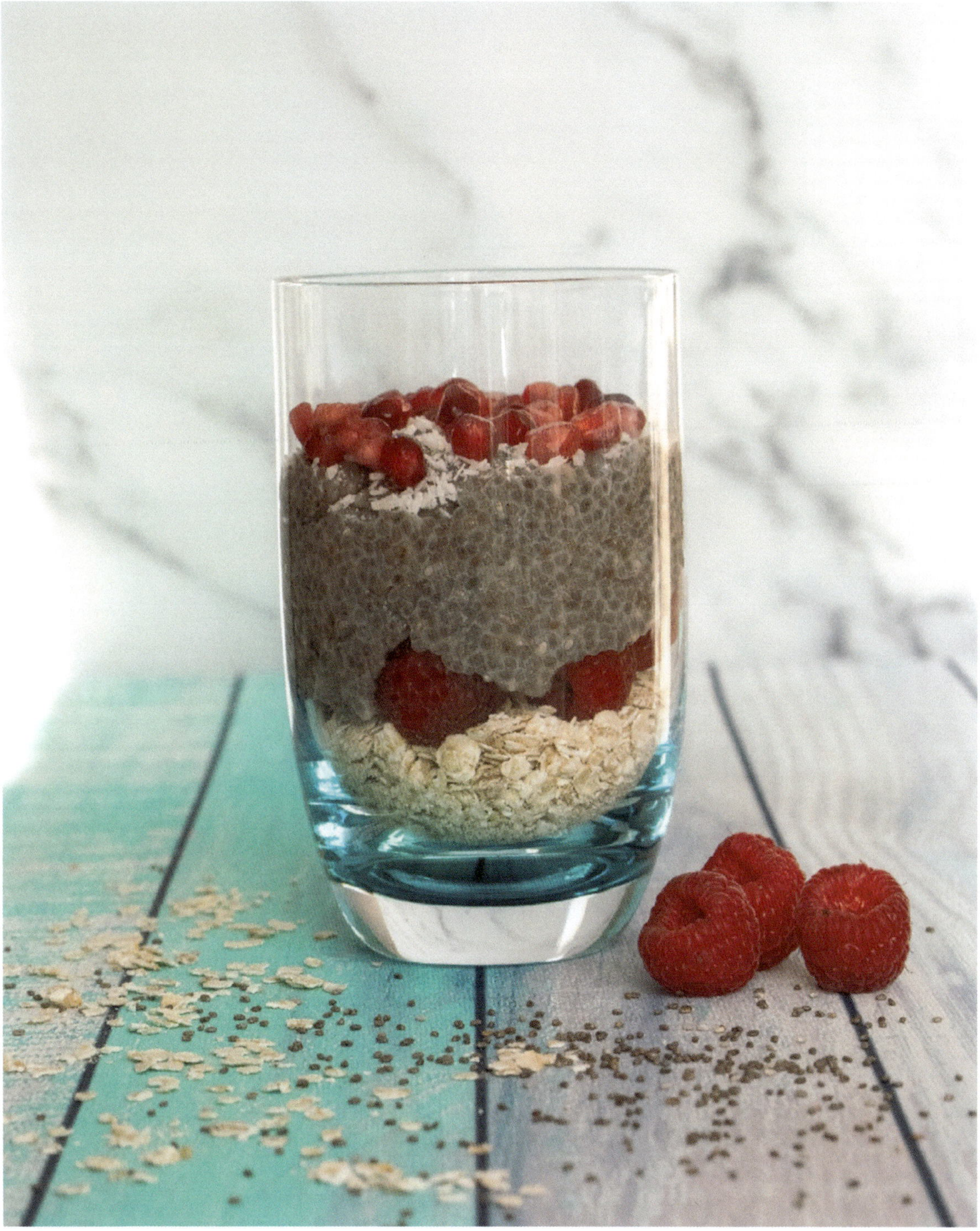

FRUITY VEGAN PANCAKES

(Per Serving) Calories 237 / Carbs 37g / Protein 11g / Fat 5g

These vegan pancakes are so light and fluffy, and extremely easy to make! The vegan protein powder helps boost your protein intake. Keep it interesting and experiment with different fruits! A real breakfast treat which takes minutes to make!

Serves 2 Prep Time 2 mins Cook Time 6 mins ## INGREDIENTS 150ml (½cup) Oat Milk 60g (2oz) Plain Flour 15g (½oz) Vegan Protein Powder (your preferred flavour) ½ tsp Baking Powder 1 tsp Ground Cinnamon 1 tsp Olive Oil 80g (2 3/4oz) Raspberries 80g (2 3/4oz) Blueberries 2 tsps Maple Syrup	## HOW TO COOK IT Add the first 5 ingredients to a blender and mix well. Heat a frying pan to a medium heat. Add half of the olive oil to the pan and then pour in half of the pancake mixture creating 2 pancakes. Cook for roughly 90 seconds per side. Keep a close eye on them so that they don't burn. Repeat this process with the remaining pancake mixture. Once cooked, plate up the pancakes, top with raspberries and blueberries and drizzle with maple syrup before serving. Note: Depending on what size you make your pancakes, you may get 6 smaller pancakes out of this mixture.

DIETICIAN'S NOTES

Using protein powder in these pancakes makes them more satiating - use a whole scoop to boost the protein per serving. Frozen fruits are ideal for pancakes, containing just as many nutrients as fresh.

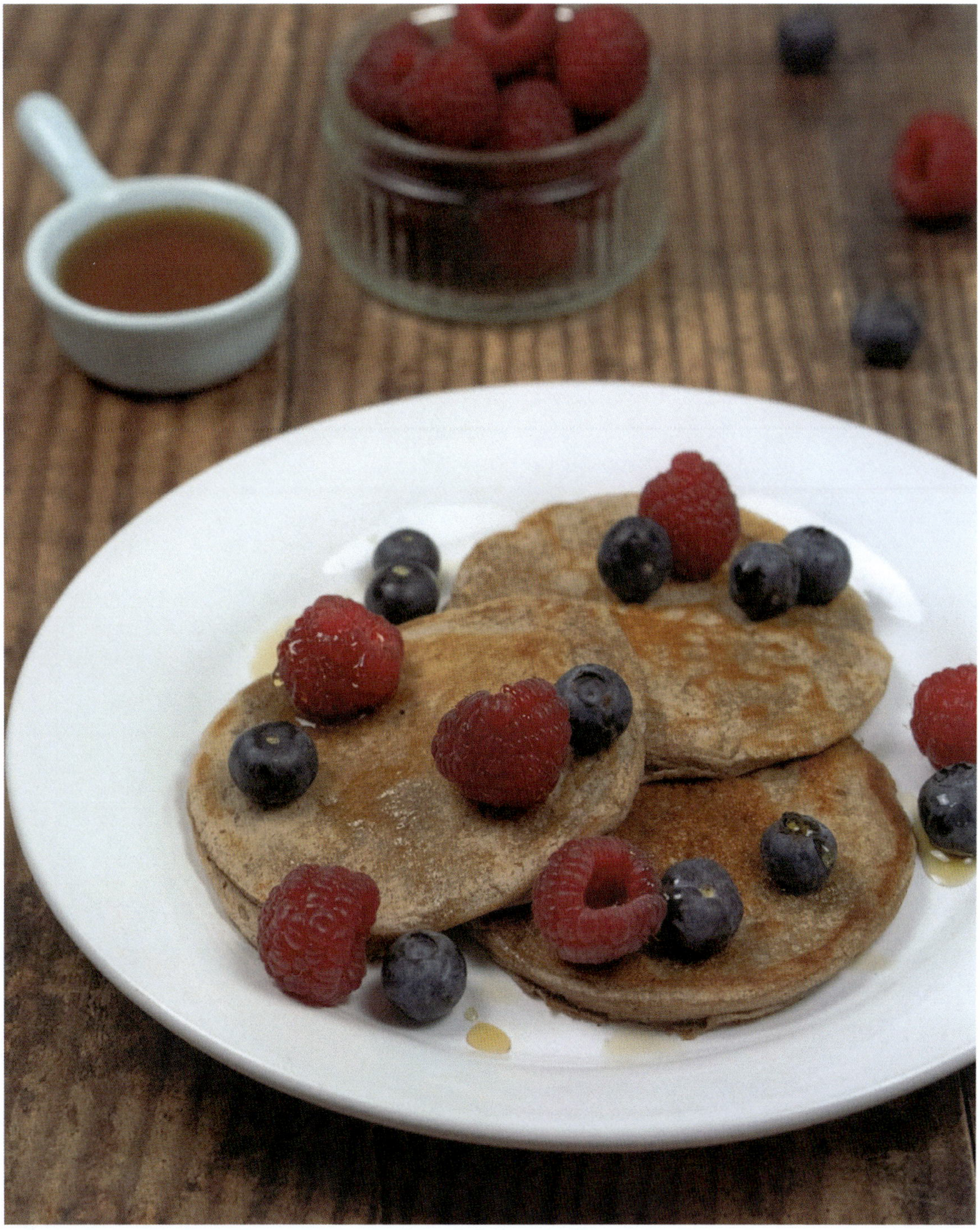

CHOCOLATEY PROTEIN SMOOTHIE

(Per Serving) Calories 308 / Carbs 36g / Protein 23g / Fat 8g

An excellent post-workout smoothie, you can't go wrong with the classic combination of chocolate and banana. Simple to make, this rich and creamy protein shake is also a great option for breakfast on-the-go.

Serves 1 Prep Time 3 mins Cook Time 0 mins ## INGREDIENTS 250ml (1 cup) Almond Chocolate 25g (3/4oz) Chocolate Vegan Protein Powder 1/2 tbsp Vegan Cocoa Powder 1/2 tbsp Flaxseeds ½ Medium Banana (peeled) A Handful of Ice Cubes	## HOW TO COOK IT Place all the ingredients into a blender and blend. Note: This drink is always best served cold. If not drunk straight away, give the drink a good shake before consuming

DIETICIAN'S NOTES

Consuming protein post-workout benefits muscle recovery. A protein shake is a convenient and tasty option and provides the recommended 25-30 grams of protein.

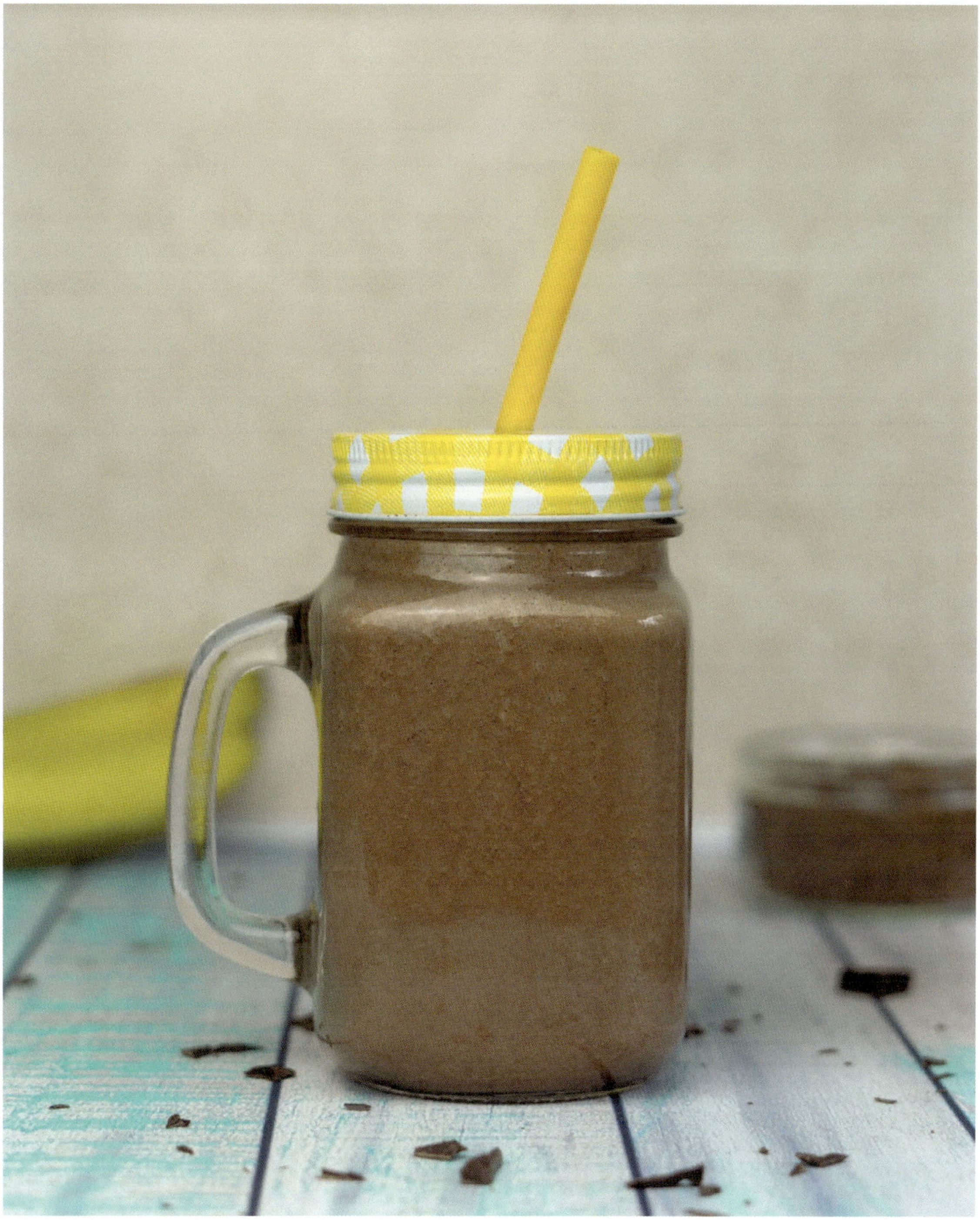

BEANS ON TOAST

(Per Serving) Calories 321 / Carbs 52g / Protein 17g / Fat 5g

This healthy twist on good old beans on toast is super-cheap to knock together and low in calories, too. Use a five bean salad or your favourite tinned beans. Flavour with chilli and basil for a tasty kick!

Serves 2 Prep Time 4 mins Cook Time 32 mins ## INGREDIENTS ½ tbsp Olive Oil ½ Red Onion (finely chopped) 1 Red Chilli (deseeded and finely chopped) 2 Garlic Cloves (finely chopped) 1 Tin Of Five Bean Salad (drained and rinsed) A Handful of Basil Leaves (roughly chopped) 1 Tin of Chopped Tomatoes Pinch of Salt Pinch of Pepper 150ml (½cup) Water 2 Wholemeal Slices of Bread	## HOW TO COOK IT Heat the olive oil in a large pan over a medium heat. Add the red onion and cook for 2-3 minutes. Then add the chilli and garlic. Give it a quick stir and cook for 30 seconds. Drain the beans, rinse and add to the pan along with the basil leaves, chopped tomatoes, salt, pepper and water. Give it a quick stir. Bring it to the boil, reduce the heat to low and cook for 25-30 minutes or until the beans have softened, stirring occasionally. If the sauce gets too dry, add a little more water. When the beans are cooked, toast the bread and plate up the dish. Optional: garnish with a little extra basil.

DIETICIAN'S NOTES

Providing a good quantity of protein and carbohydrates, this dish would be ideal post-workout. Cooked tomatoes also contain a compound known as lycopene, which helps with muscle recovery.

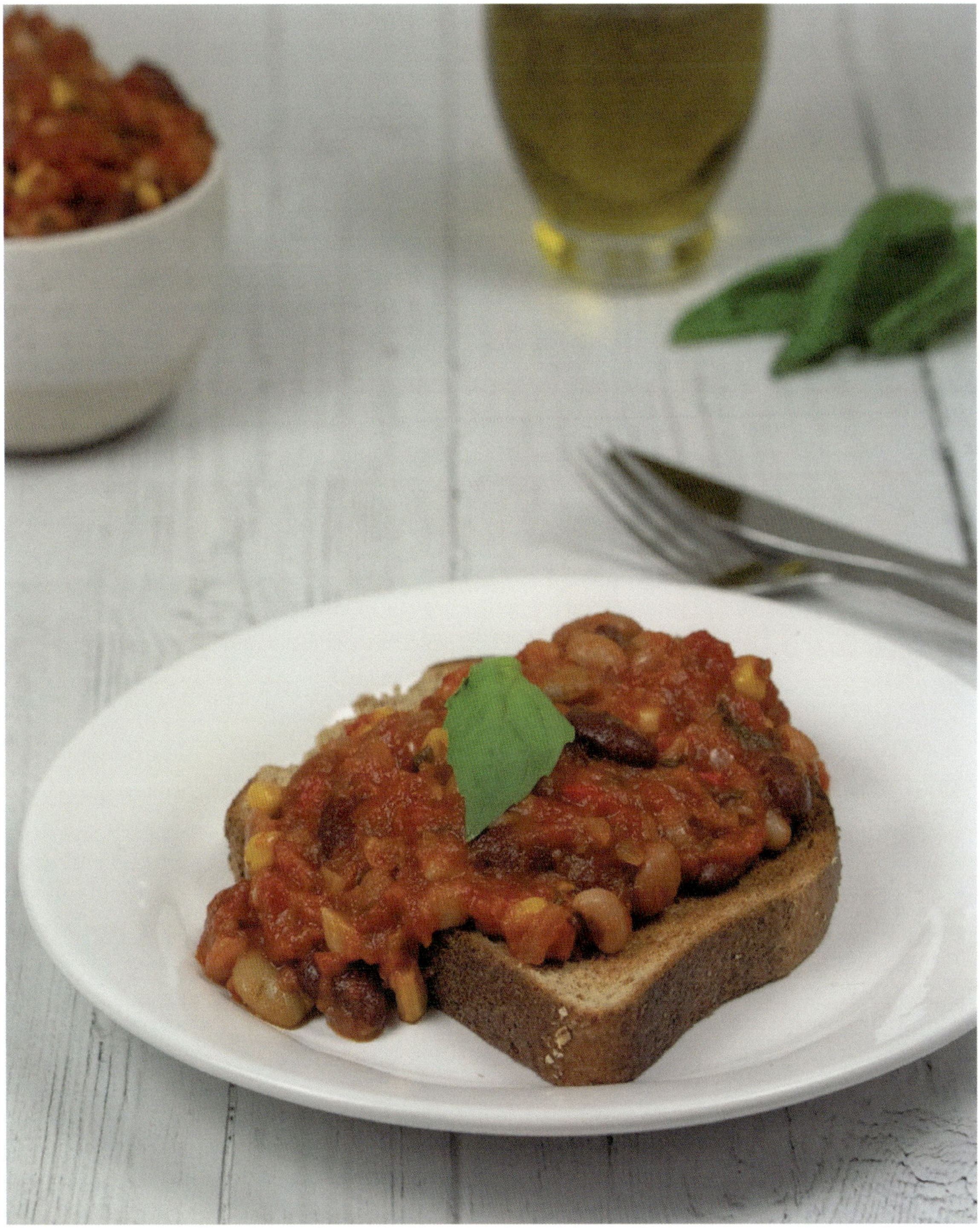

SWEET POTATO QUESADILLAS

(Per Serving) Calories 411 / Carbs 59g / Protein 10g / Fat 15g

Crispy on the outside and gooey on the inside, these vegan quesadillas are perfect for a quick lunch or dinner (they're ready in just ten minutes). Sweet potato, haricot beans and avocado combine with spices to create a Mexican meal to remember!

Serves 2 Prep Time 8 mins Cook Time 10 mins ## INGREDIENTS 1/2 tbsp Olive Oil 200g (7oz) Sweet Potato (peeled and grated) 1 tbsp Maple Syrup 1tsp Smoked Chipotle Chilli Paste 1/2 Red Chilli (deseeded and finely chopped) Pinch of Salt Pinch of Pepper 1/2 Tin (200g / 7oz) (non-drained weight) Harico Beans (drained and rinsed) 1/2 Avocado (stoned, peeled and mashed) 1/2 Lime (juiced) 2 Corn Tortillas	## HOW TO COOK IT Add the olive oil to a deep frying pan and heat over a medium heat. Add the sweet potato to the pan along with the maple syrup, smoked chipotle chilli paste, red chilli, salt and pepper. Mix it all together and cook for 4-5 minutes until the potato softens Once softened, add to a large mixing bowl. Drain the Harico beans, rinse them under the tap and add to the mixing bowl. Mash until they are mixed in with the sweet potato mixture. Add the avocado to the mixture along with the lime juice and mash it all together one last time. Heat a large frying pan over a medium heat. When hot, lay 1 tortilla flat into the pan. Spoon in half of the mixture and spread over half of the tortilla. Fold it over to create a sandwich. Cook until the tortilla is golden brown. Flip it over and cook the other side. Keep this tortilla warm while you prepare the other tortilla. Extra: This dish is excellent when served with a side salad

DIETICIAN'S NOTES

Haricot beans are a great source of folate, which helps to prevent tiredness and fatigue. Avocados and beans are rich in soluble fibre, which can help regulate cholesterol levels.

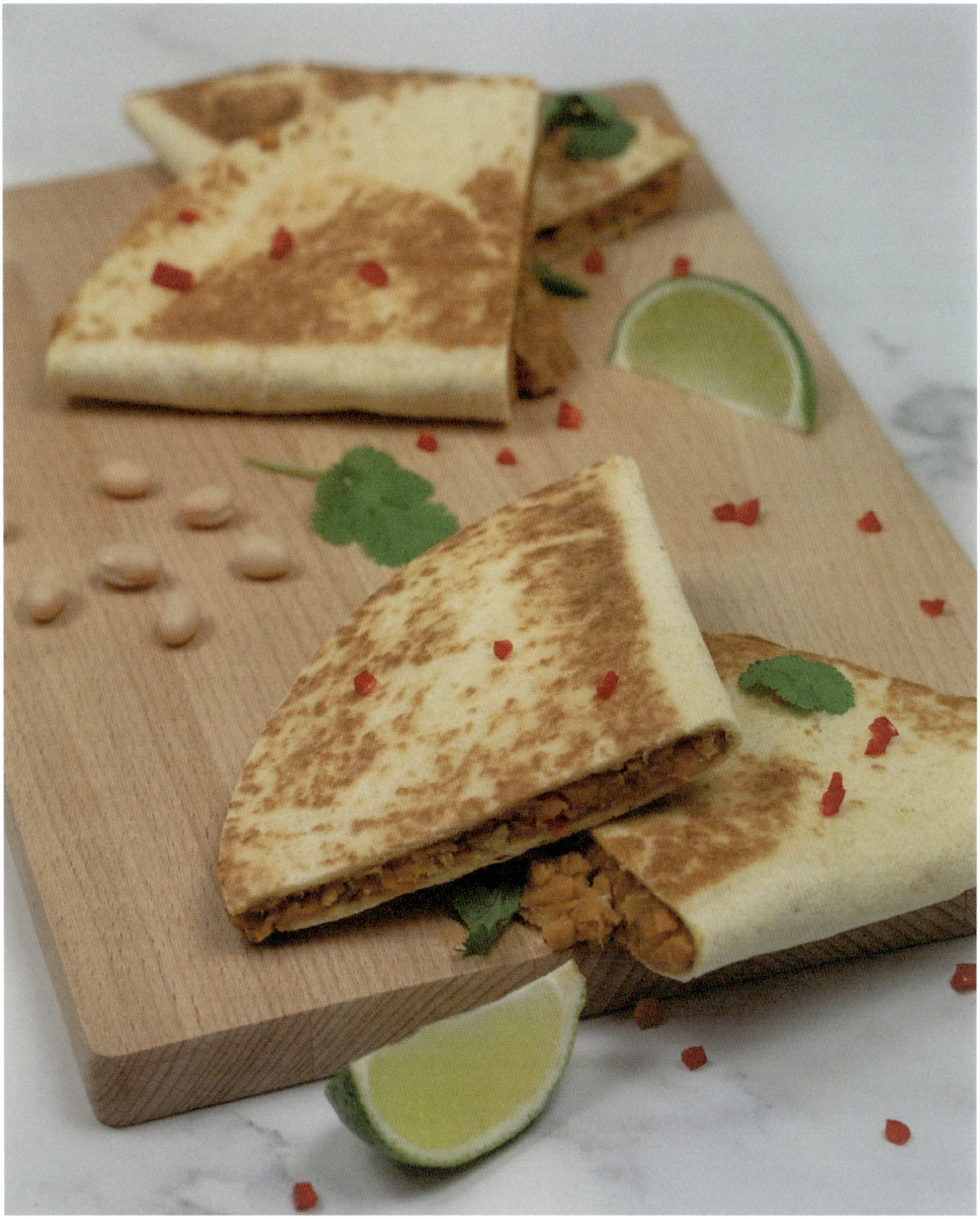

SUPER GREENS SALAD

(Per Serving) Calories 360 / Carbs 39g / Protein 15g / Fat 16g

Packed with nutritious grains, greens and vegetables, this salad is full of feel-good flavours. Add soy sauce and lime for an Asian kick!

Serves 2
Prep Time 5 mins
Cook Time 30 mins

INGREDIENTS

200g (7oz) Sweet Potato (peeled and cut into small chunks)
1 tbsp Olive Oil
Pinch of Salt & Pepper
105ml (1/2cup) Boiling Water
1/2 Vegetable Stock Cube 35g (1 1/4oz) - Quinoa (dry weight)
100g (3 1/2oz) Kale (thick stalks removed)
100g (3 1/2oz) Soya Edamame Beans
10g (1/4oz) Sunflower Seed Kernels
10g (1/4oz) Pumpkin Seeds 1 tbsp Light Soy Sauce
1/2 Lime (juiced)

HOW TO COOK IT

Preheat the oven to 200°C (390°F) and boil the kettle while you prepare the sweet potato.

Add the sweet potato to a non-stick baking tray. Add half the oil and a pinch of salt and pepper. Mix well and place in the oven for 25-30 minutes, until soft and golden brown.

In a small saucepan add 105ml (1/2cup) of boiling water and the vegetable stock cube. Dissolve the stock cube and then add the quinoa. Cook for 10 minutes on a medium heat. Then cover the pan, reduce the heat down and simmer for 15 minutes, stirring occasionally.

Fill a large pan with boiling water, add the kale and cook for 90secs, then place the kale in ice water to stop it cooking anymore.

Add the Edamame beans to a bowl and pour boiling water over them. Leave them in the water for 10 minutes, before draining them.

When the quinoa is done, most of the water should have been absorbed. Drain off any excess water and leave to stand for 5 minutes.

Meanwhile, add the sunflower seeds and pumpkin seeds to a pan over a medium heat and toast them. The seeds will start popping when they are ready. Make sure you don't burn them.

Add the quinoa, edamame beans, sweet potato, toasted seeds, remaining olive oil, soy sauce, lime, salt and pepper to a large mixing bowl and mix well.

Drain the kale and add to the plate. Then spoon the quinoa mixture on top of the kale and serve..

DIETICIAN'S NOTES

Certain fats contained in seeds have been linked with a lower risk of heart disease. Together with the olive oil and colourful vegetables, this ticks the boxes for a heart-healthy dish.

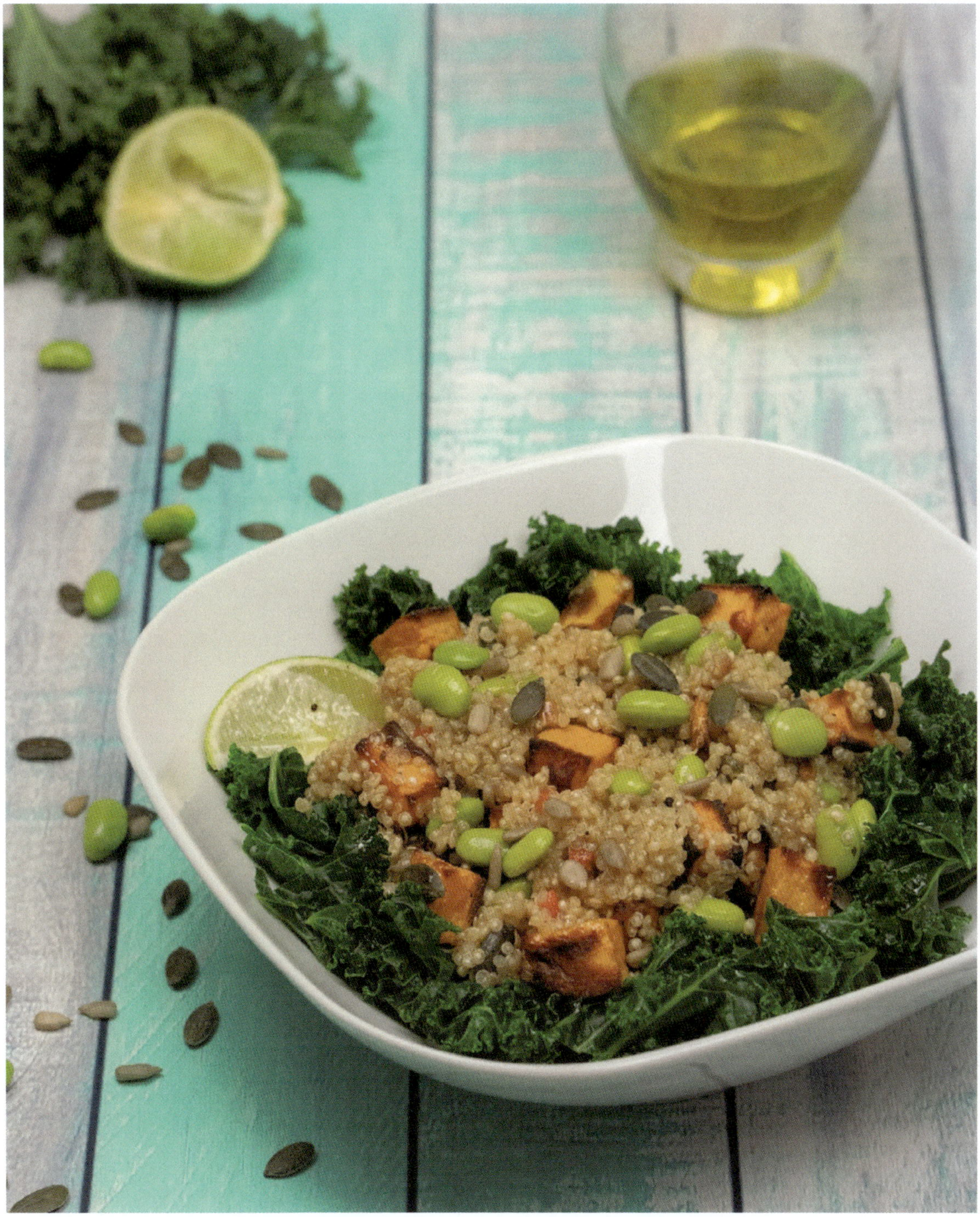

ROAST BUTTERNUT SQUASH & SPINACH SALAD

(Per Serving) Calories 240 / Carbs 26g / Protein 7g / Fat 12g

This vegan and gluten-free salad features red peppers, cherry tomatoes and a light balsamic dressing. Perfect as a starter or a light meal, it's easy to prepare, plus tastes delicious and looks amazing!

Serves 2
Prep Time 4 mins
Cook Time 30 mins

INGREDIENTS

400g (14oz) Butternut Squash (peeled, remove the seeds and cut into 2cm chunks)
2 tbsp Olive Oil
1 tsp Smoked Paprika Pinch of Salt & Pepper 100g (3 1/2oz) Cucumber (peeled, cut in half, lengthways, deseeded with a spoon and thinly sliced)
100g (3 1/2oz) Cherry Tomatoes (cut into quarters)
70g (2 1/2oz) Celery (cut in half, lengthways. Then thinly slice)
100g (3 1/2oz) Red Bell Peppers (core removed, deseeded and cut into chunks)
100g (3 1/2oz) Spinach
15g (1/2oz) Sunflower Seeds
1 1/2 tbsp Balsamic Vinegar

HOW TO COOK IT

Preheat the oven to 220°C (430°F).

Once you have prepared the butternut squash, add it to a non-stick baking tray. Add half of the olive oil, smoked paprika, salt and pepper and mix well before placing in the oven and cooking for about 30 minutes (they are cooked when soft and golden brown).

While the butternut squash is cooking, grab a large mixing bowl and add the cucumber, tomatoes, celery, red bell peppers and spinach to the bowl and mix (you may need to add the spinach in gradually, depending on the size of the mixing bowl).

Toast the Sunflower seeds in a pan over a medium heat. This should take a couple of minutes to slightly brown, but ensure you don't burn them.

Add the sunflower seeds to the mixing bowl and put to one side.

Make the salad dressing by adding the remaining olive oil, balsamic vinegar and a pinch of pepper together. Don't add the dressing until you serve up.

Finish off the salad by adding the cooked butternut squash. Toss the salad and serve.

DIETICIAN'S NOTES

Butternut squash is a great source of vitamins A & C, which are important for immune function. This salad is a great way to boost vegetabkle intake, providing three of the recommended 5-A-DAY.

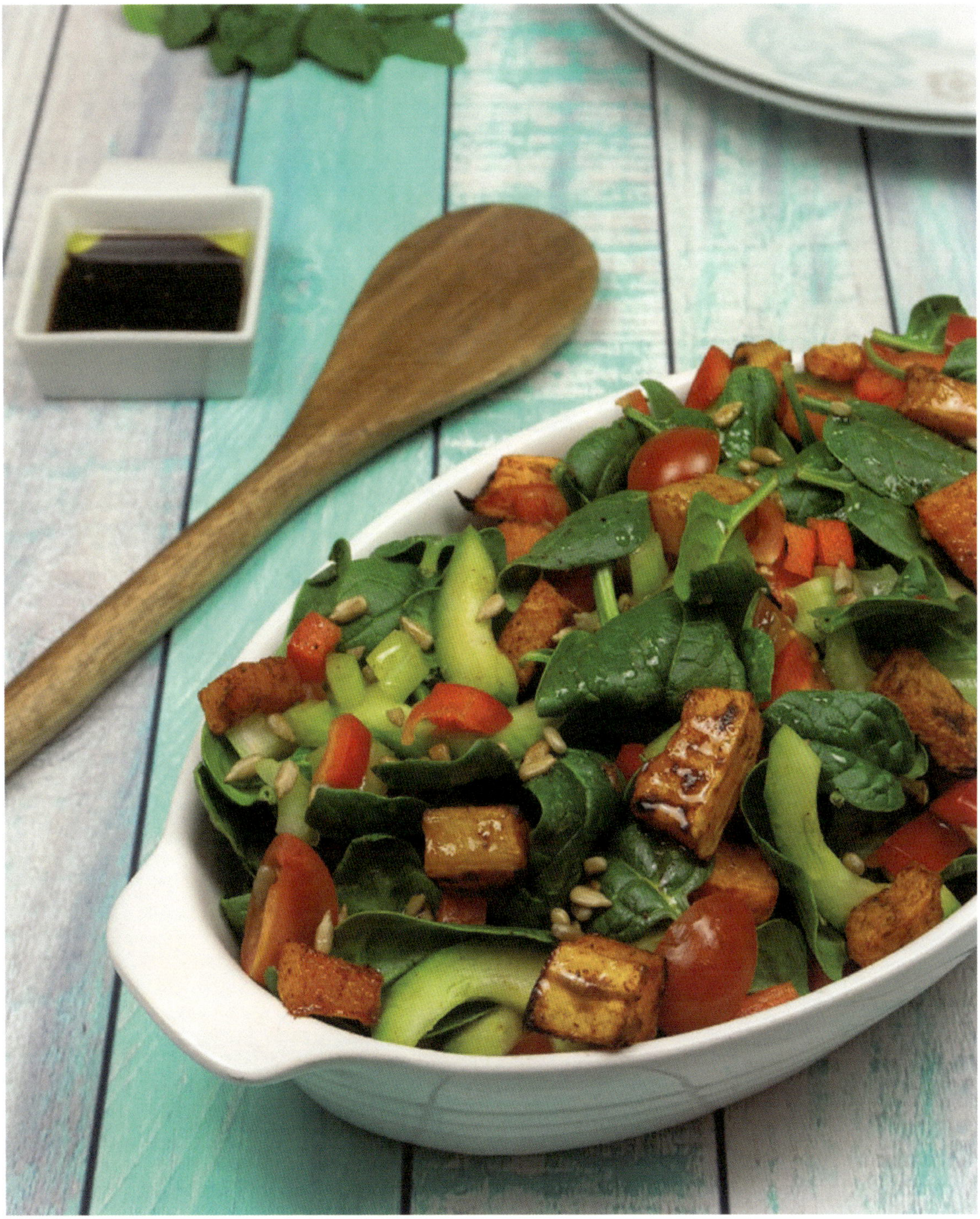

CRISPY AUBERGINE SANDWICH

(Per Serving) Calories 314 / Carbs 37g / Protein 10g / Fat 14g

There are so many delicious flavours and textures in this hearty sandwich - the buttery avocado, juicy tomato and the sweet aubergine complement each other perfectly. This is a great lunch option.

Serves 2 Prep Time 5 mins Cook Time 35 mins ## INGREDIENTS 1 tbsp Olive Oil 1tbsp Light Soy Sauce 1 tsp Maple Syrup 1/2 tsp Smoked Paprika 150g (5 1/4oz) Aubergine (Eggplant) (Cut into quaters, lengthways. Cut each quater into strips) 2Lettuce Leaves 1 Large Tomato (cut into thin slices) 1/2 Avocado (stoned, peeled and thinly sliced) 4 Slices of Wholemeal Bread (toasted)	## HOW TO COOK IT Preheat the oven to 150°C (300°F). In a small mixing bowl, create your marinade by adding the olive oil, soy sauce, maple syrup and smoked paprika together. Give it a quick stir and put to one side. Line a baking tray with greaseproof paper. Place your aubergine (eggplant) strips onto a baking tray. With a brush, coat the aubergine (eggplant) strips with the marinade and place in the oven for 30-35 minutes, turning halfway through. If you like them crispy, cook for slightly longer. While the aubergine (eggplant) strips are cooking, prepare your lettuce, tomatoes and avocado. Once the aubergine (eggplant) strips are cooked, toast your bread. Layer the sandwich together like this: toast, lettuce, tomato, aubergine (eggplant), avocado, toast. Time to tuck in....enjoy!

DIETICIAN'S NOTES

Avocados are a great source of healthy fats and contain a range of nutrients including folate, which is important for healthy red blood cells. With wholemeal bread, this sandwich is a good source of fibre. Add some sliced tofu for an extra protein boost.

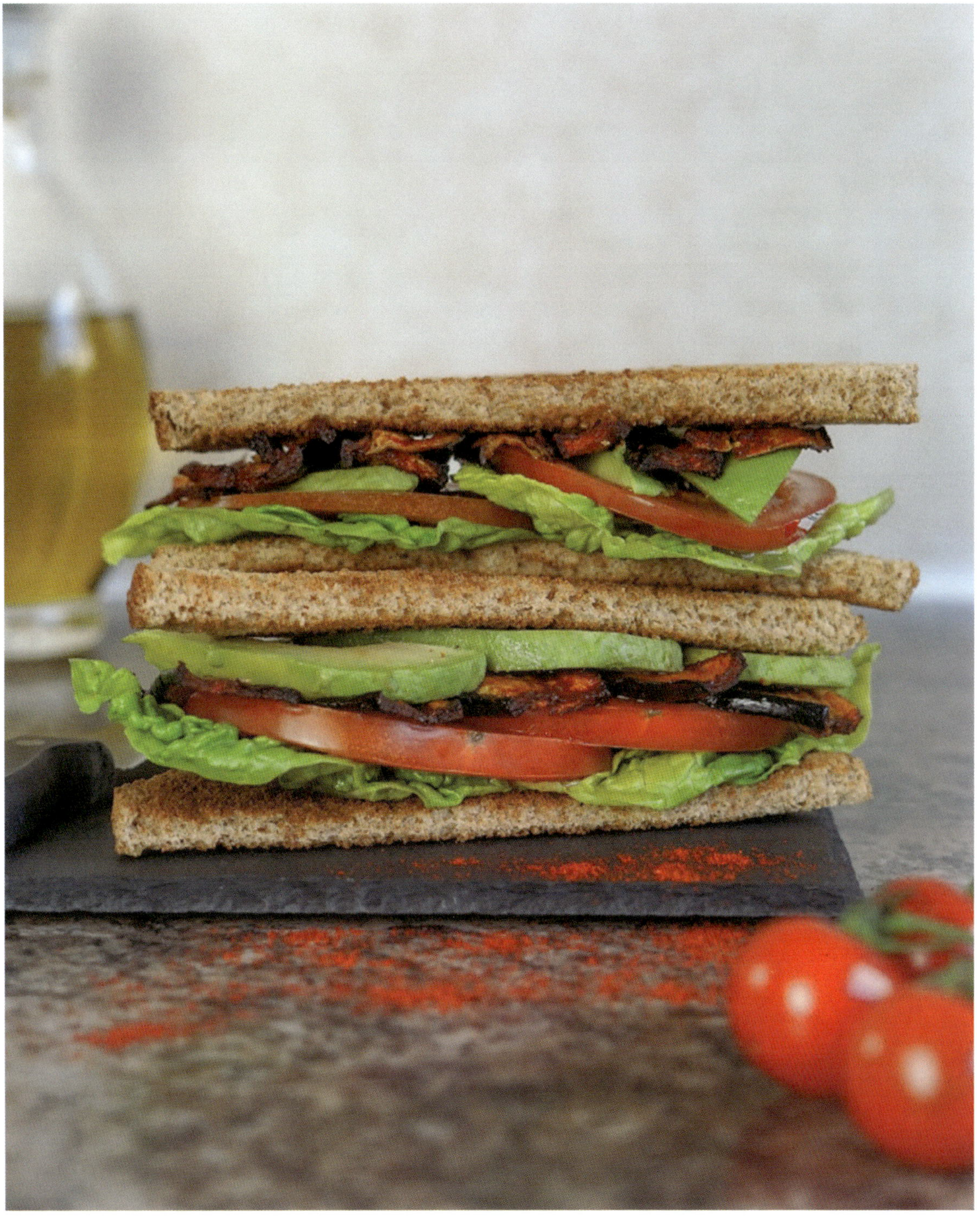

CHILLI, MANGO AND BLACK BEAN SALAD

(Per Serving) Calories 286 / Carbs 37g / Protein 12g / Fat 10g

Ready in just ten minutes, this colourful salad combines veggies and fruit with chilli and lime for a sweet, spicy kick. It keeps well and is a great option if you're into meal prepping.

Serves 2 Prep Time 10 mins Cook Time 0 mins ## INGREDIENTS 100g (3 1/2oz) Red Bell Pepper (core removed and roughly chopped) 100g (3 1/2oz) Cucumber (cut in half lengthways, remove the seeds and slice diagonally) 100g (3 1/2oz) Cherry Tomatoes (cut in half) 2 Spring Onions (Scallion) (remove the ends and thinly slice) 1/2 Avocado (stoned, peeled and cut in chunks) 1/2 Red Chilli (deseeded and finely chopped) Handful of Coriander (Cilantro) (stalks removed and roughly chopped) 150g (5 1/4oz) Mango (peeled, stone removed and cut into chunks) 1 x 400g (14oz) Tin - Black Beans (drained and washed) 1 Lime (zest & juice)	## HOW TO COOK IT Before you start chopping up the ingredients, please ensure you wash all the ingredients that don't need peeling. Place all the ingredients in a large mixing bowl, finishing with the lime juice. Mix it all together and serve.

DIETICIAN'S NOTES

You'll tick off four of your 5-A-DAY with this salad. With fruits, vegetables and beans, it's a rich source of vitamins, minerals and fibre. The fats from the avocado actually help your body absorb more of the vitamins too, making this a great combo.

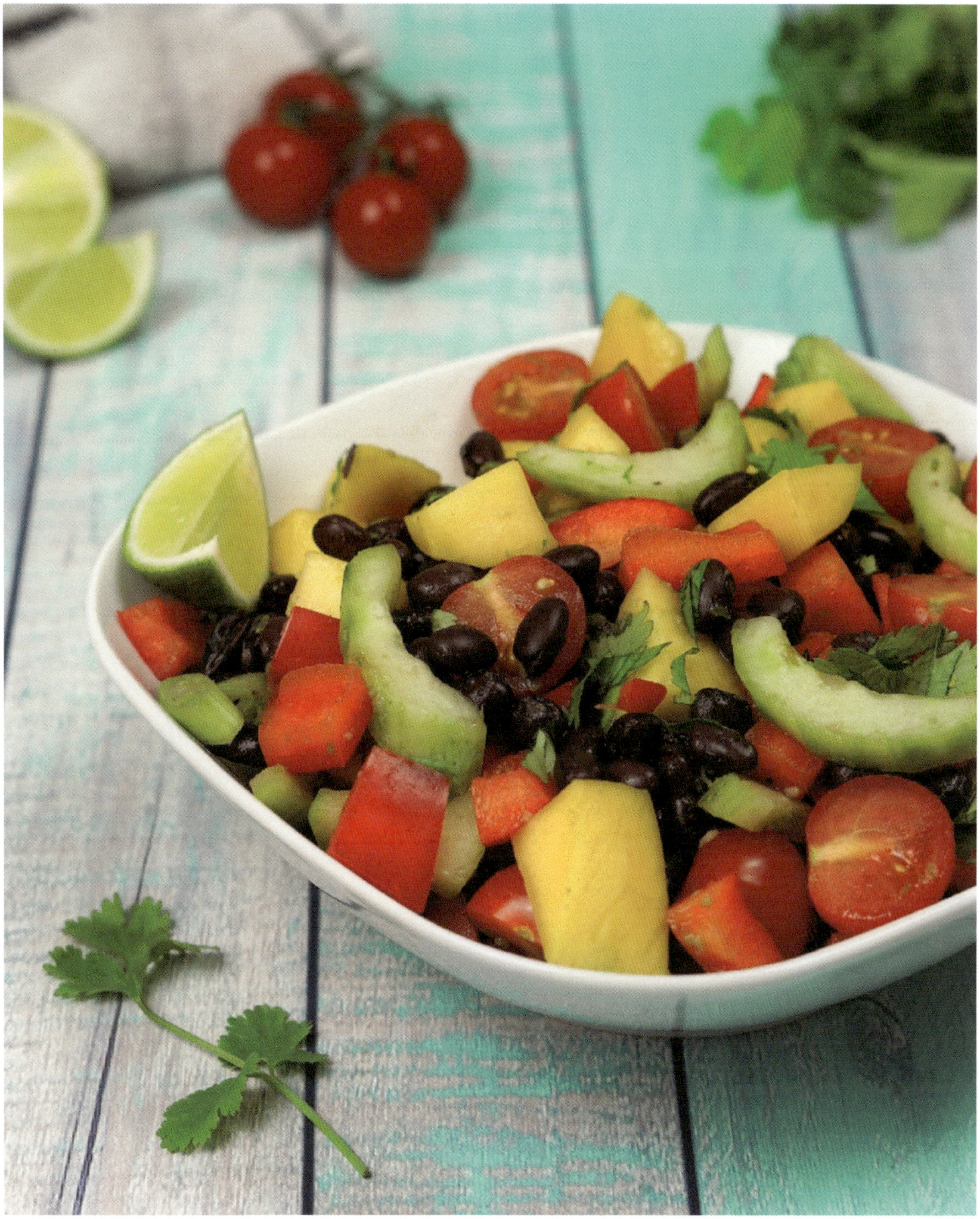

ORZO & SPINACH SOUP

(Per Serving) Calories 317 / Carbs 47g / Protein 12g / Fat 9g

A hearty vegan soup featuring orzo pasta, spinach and lentils which is sure to keep you full all afternoon or evening. A variety of herbs and tasty vegetables adds real flavour. Top with chilli flakes to add some heat.

Serves 2
Prep Time 6 mins
Cook Time 20 mins

INGREDIENTS

1 Vegetable Stock Cube
1200ml (5cups) Boiling Water
2tbsp Olive Oil 1 White Onion (peeled & finely chopped)
1 Carrot (ends removed, peeled, halve and quarter lengthways and finely chop)
2 Celery Sticks (ends removed, halved lengthways and finely chopped)
3 Garlic Cloves (peeled & finely chopped) 1 Can Chopped Tomatoes 100g (3 1/2oz) Orza Pasta
50g (1 3/4oz) Red Split Lentils
1/2 tsp Dried Thyme
1/2 tsp Dried Rosemary 1/2 tsp Dried Oregano Pinch of Salt & Pepper 100g (3 1/2oz) Spinach
Optional Topping: Chilli Flakes

HOW TO COOK IT

Dissolve the vegetable stock cube in the boiling water.

Add the olive oil to large non-stick pan and heat to a medium heat.

Add the onions to the pan and cook for 3 minutes. Make sure the onions don't burn.

Then add the carrot, celery and garlic. Cook for 3 more minutes.

Add the vegetable stock and the remaining ingredients apart from the spinach and chilli flakes.

Turn the heat up and bring to the boil and then reduce the heat and simmer for 12 minutes, stirring occasionally. Then add the spinach, stir it in and cook for 2 minutes, until it has wilted.

Serve up the soup.

If you like a little heat, sprinkle some chilli flakes on top before serving.

DIETICIAN'S NOTES

Containing vitamin and fibre rich vegetables and lentils, this soup should be a filling choice that will score two of your 5-A-DAY. Top with a spoonful of hummus or some crumbled tofu for more of a protein kick.

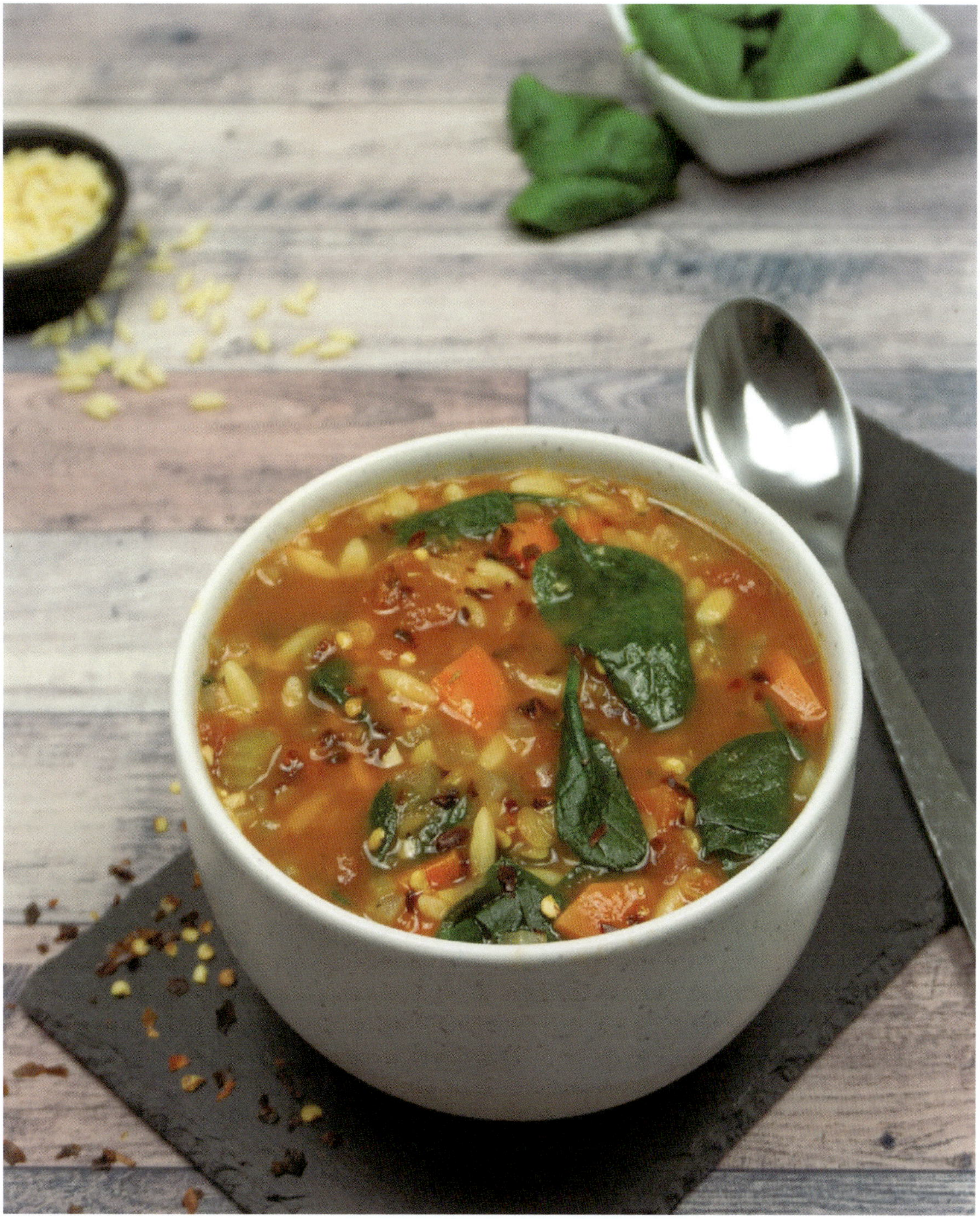

FALAFELS WITH MEDITERRANEAN COUSCOUS SALAD

(Per Serving) Calories 325 / Carbs 49g / Protein 12g / Fat 9g

Ready in just ten minutes, this no-cook taste of the Middle East is perfect for a mid-week lunch or dinner. Add fragrant harissa (chilli) paste to your falafel mix for an extra kick. Serve your homemade falafels with filling couscous and salad for a mezzo style meal.

Serves 2
Prep Time 10 mins
Cook Time 14 mins

INGREDIENTS

120g (4 1/4oz) Couscous (dry weight)
1 Vegetable Stock Cube 200ml (1 cup) Boiling Water 1/2 tsp Turmeric
200g (7oz) Canned Chickpeas (non drained weight) (drained & rinsed)
1/2 Red Onion (roughly chopped)
1 Garlic Clove (roughly chopped)
1 Heaped tbsp Flat-Leaf Parsley (roughly chopped)
1/2 tsp Ground Cumin
1/2 tsp Ground Coriander (Cilantro)
1/4 tsp Harissa Paste or Chilli Powder
1 tbsp Plain Flour 1/2 Lemon Zest
Pinch of Salt & Pepper
1 1/2 tbsp Olive Oil 100g (3 1/2oz) Cherry Tomatoes (cut into quarters)
100g (3 1/2oz) Cucumber (cut into quarters lengthways & then roughly chopped)
1 tbsp Lemon Juice

HOW TO COOK IT

Add the couscous into a bowl. Dissolve the vegetable stock cube in the boiling water. When dissolved, add the turmeric, give it a quick mix and then pour over the couscous. Give it one last quick stir, cover with a tea towel and put to one side to allow the couscous to absorb the vegetable stock — roughly 10 minutes.

Meanwhile, add the chickpeas, red onion, garlic, parsley, ground cumin, ground coriander (cilantro), harissa paste (or chilli powder), plain flour, lemon zest and a pinch of salt and pepper to a blender and whizz the ingredients together.

Once blended, wet your hands, so the mixture doesn't stick and start to roll the mixture into about 6-8 small balls (these are your falafels).

Add 1 tbsp oil to a large frying pan and heat to a medium heat. Once hot, add the falafels to the pan and cook for about 8-10 minutes. They should be a nice golden brown all over when done.

While the falafels are cooking, prepare the tomatoes and cucumber and add them to a mixing bowl. Add the lemon juice, remaining olive oil and a pinch of salt. Give it a quick mix and leave to one side for a minute.

Now fluff up the couscous with a fork.

Plate up the couscous, salad and falafels and enjoy.

DIETICIAN'S NOTES

Chickpeas are a great source of fibre and vitamin B6, which helps us release energy from food. This is a vegetable packed meal, containing lots of antioxidants. If you want to increase the protein content, serve with a spoonful of hummus or a tzatziki made with soya yoghurt.

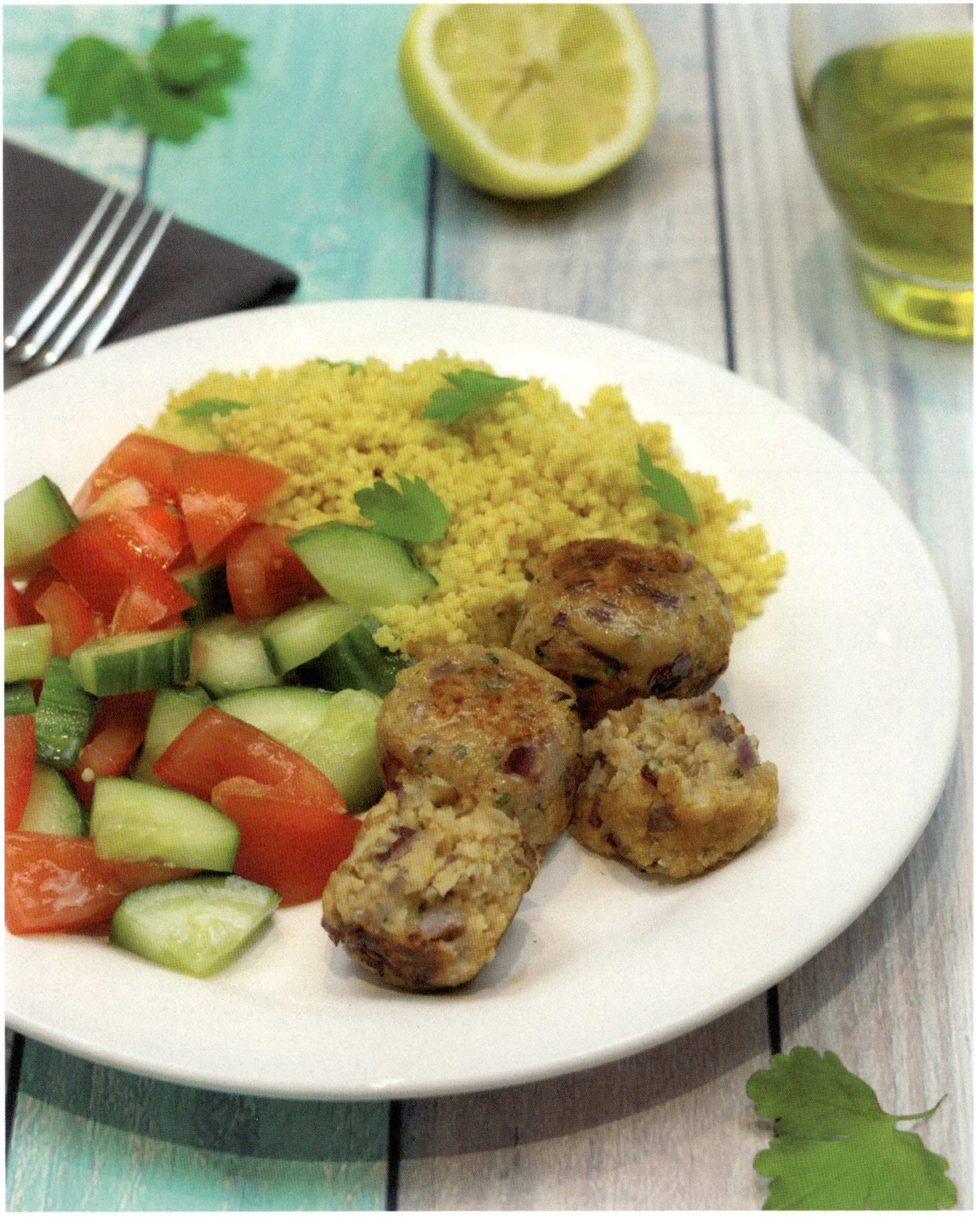

QUINOA & CHICKPEA SALAD

(Per Serving) Calories 361 / Carbs 37g / Protein 15g / Fat 17g

Quinoa makes a great salad base, but it does need some big flavours - here it's teamed with tahini, coriander, lemon juice and mustard, veggies and pulses for a satisfying lunch or light meal.

Serves 2 Prep Time 2 mins Cook Time 25 mins ## INGREDIENTS 100g (3 1/2oz) Dried Quinoa 240g (8 1/2oz) Tin Cooked Chickpeas (drained weight) 3/4 tsp Dijon Mustard 1/2 tbsp Tahini 1 tbsp Lemon Juice 20ml Water Pinch of salt Pinch of Pepper 1/2 Small Red Onion (finely chopped) 15 Cherry Tomatoes (halved) 1/2 Medium Avocado (diced) 10g (1/4oz) Coriander (Cilantro) (roughly chopped)	## HOW TO COOK IT Boil the kettle. Meanwhile, rinse the quinoa under cold water. Then add it to a saucepan and pour the boiling water over the quinoa. Cook it according to the package directions. Then add 50g of chickpeas to a food processor or blender along with Dijon Mustard, tahini, lemon juice, water and a pinch of salt and pepper. Blend the mixture until it becomes a creamy consistency. This is your salad sauce. Once done, put to one side. Add the remaining chickpeas to a large mixing bowl along with the quinoa, red onion, cherry tomatoes, avocado and coriander (cilantro). Plate up the salad and serve the dressing separately to pour over when you are ready to eat.

DIETICIAN'S NOTES

Teaming quinoa and chickpeas elevates the protein and fibre content of this simple salad, making it a filling choice. You'll also benefit from heart-healthy fats from the avocado and tahini.

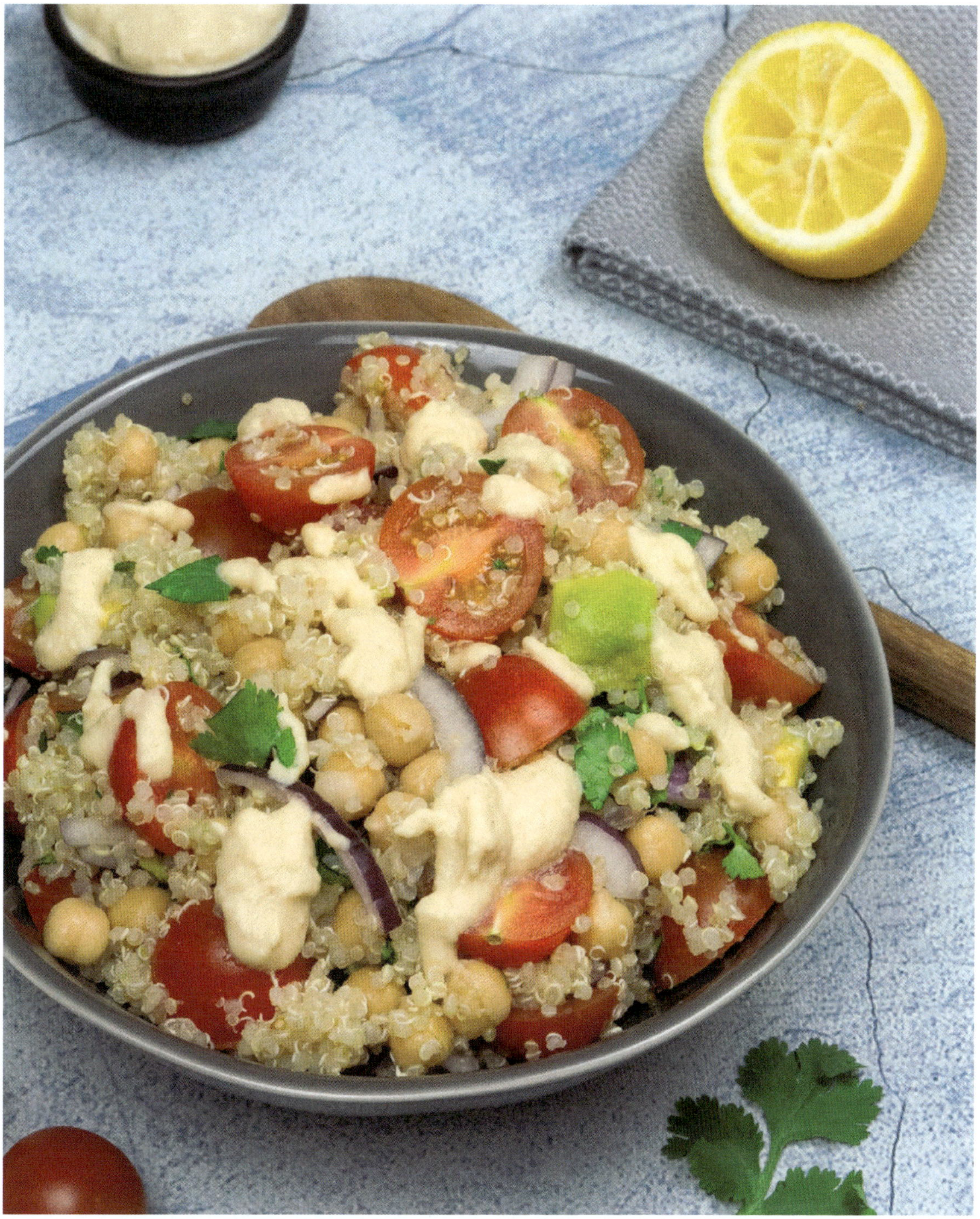

CURRIED CHICKPEAS ON BAKED SWEET POTATO

(Per Serving) Calories 361 / Carbs 57g / Protein 13g / Fat 9g

Vegan comfort food at its best! Curried chickpeas bring heat and bold flavour which goes really well with the sweetness of the potato. This creamy, satisfying dish is an easy weeknight meal, or a filling weekend lunch.

Serves 2
Prep Time 10 mins
Cook Time 30 mins

INGREDIENTS

300g (10 1/2oz) Sweet Potato
(cut in half lengthways)
1 tbsp Olive Oil
Pinch of Salt & Pepper 1/2 Medium Onion
(finely chopped)
1/2 tsp Turmeric
1 tsp Ground Cumin
1tsp Ground Coriander (Cilantro)
2tsp Garam Masala
1tsp Mild Curry Powder 3 tbsp Water
Thumb Sized Piece of Ginger (peeled and finely chopped or grated)
2 Garlic Cloves
(peeled and finely chopped)
50g (1 3/4oz) Red Bell Pepper
(roughly chopped)
400g (14oz) Tinned Chickpeas (undrained weight)
(drained and rinsed)
1 Lemon (juiced)
50g (1 3/4oz) Cherry Tomatoes
(cut in half)
Coriander (Cilantro)
(for Garnish)

HOW TO COOK IT

Preheat the oven to 200°C (390°F).

Once you have cut the sweet potato in half, use a fork and prick the flat surface a few times to help the sweet potato cook quicker. Then add half of the olive oil and a pinch of salt and pepper.

Place in the oven and cook for 30 minutes or until the sweet potato is cooked through.

In a large frying pan, add the remaining olive oil over a medium heat.

Add the onions and cook for 3 minutes so that they are slightly softened but not browned.

Now add the 5 spices and 1 tbsp of water. This will help turn the spices into more of a paste. Give it a quick stir.

Add the ginger, garlic and red bell peppers - stir once again. Add the chickpeas and lemon juice, stir and cook for 5 minutes.

Finally, add the tomatoes and 2 tablespoons of water to loosen the curry paste and cook for 3 more minutes.

Once the sweet potato is cooked, add to a plate and top with the curried chickpeas and finish with a garnish of coriander (cilantro).

DIETICIAN'S NOTES

Spices have powerful antioxidant effects in the body and are a great way to add flavour to a dish without adding extra sugar, salt or fat. This vegetable combo is rich in fibre too

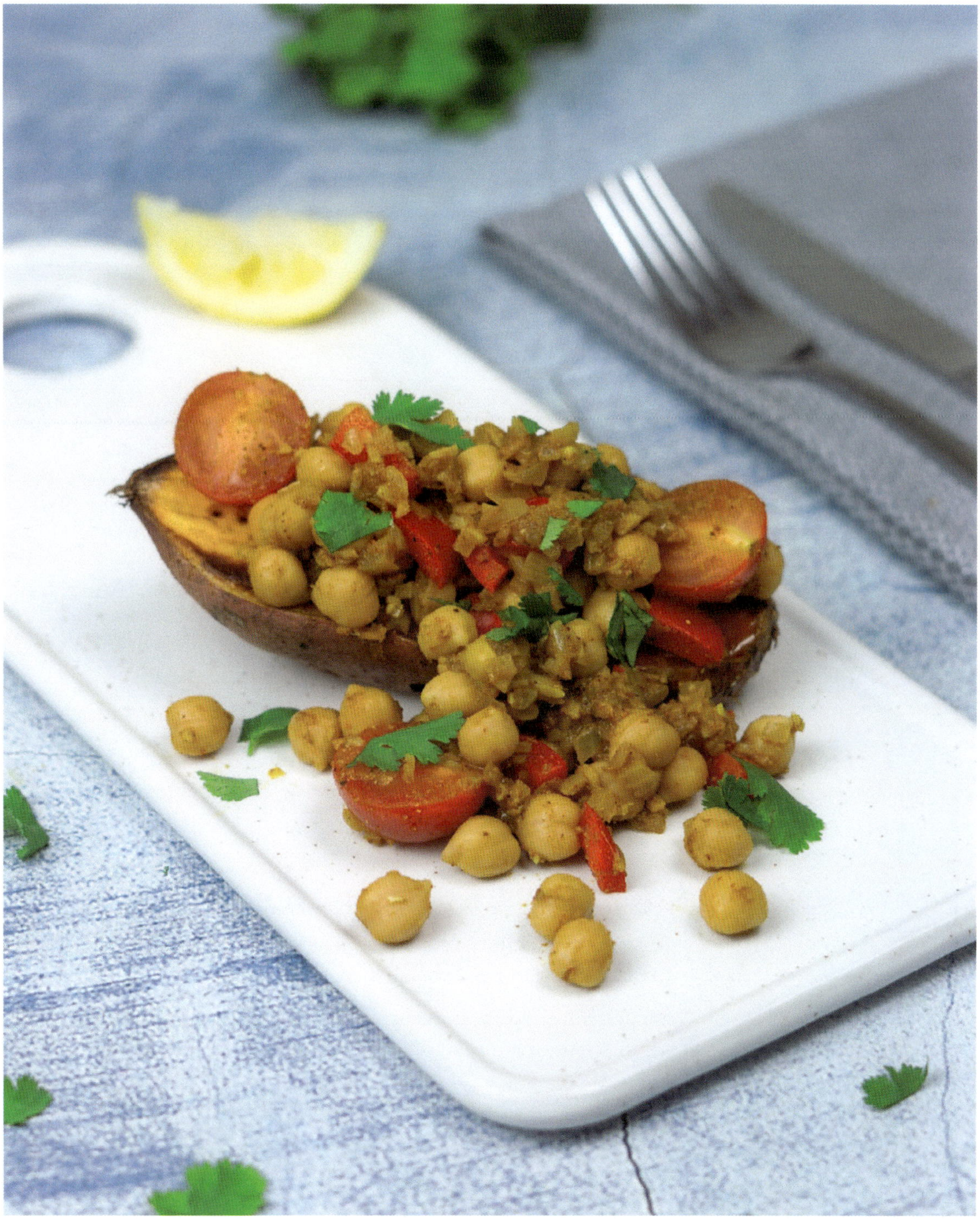

LASAGNE SOUP

(Per Serving) Calories 298 / Carbs 50g / Protein 11g / Fat 6g

Get all the flavours of a hearty, comforting lasagne in a delicious vegan soup! It's a great way to warm up on a cold day, and the flavours are incredible! Add vegan pesto for even more flavour.

Serves 2
Prep Time 5 mins
Cook Time 20 mins

INGREDIENTS

1. tsp Olive Oil
1/2 Brown Onion
(finely chopped)
2. Garlic Cloves
(finely chopped)
50g (1 3/4oz) Zucchini
(cut into small chunks)
50g (1 3/4oz) Red Bell Peppers
(cut into small chunks)
50g (1 3/4oz) Carrots (peeled and cut into small chunks)
32g (1oz) Red Split Lentils
(uncooked weight)
120ml (1/2 cup) Tomato Passata
200g (7oz) Chopped Tomatoes
170ml (3/4cup) Boiling Water
1 tsp Italian Seasoning
(or a pinch of basil, oregano, parsley, thyme, sage and rosemary)
Pinch of Salt and Pepper
100g (3 1/2oz) Lasagne Sheets
(broken into small pieces)
70g (2 1/2oz) cup packed spinach
1 tsp Vegan Pesto

HOW TO COOK IT

Add the olive oil to a large non-stick pan.

Add the onion and cook for 3 minutes.

Then add the garlic and cook for 30 seconds.

Now add the zucchini, red bell pepper, carrot, red split lentils, tomato passata, chopped tomatoes, boiling water, Italian seasoning, finishing with a pinch of salt and pepper. Mix it all together.

Bring to the boil and then turn the heat down and simmer for 15 minutes.

Meanwhile, cut the lasagne sheets into rough lengths (they don't need to be perfect)

Add the lasagne sheets to a saucepan of boiling water and cook as per the instructions on the packet.

When done, drain the lasagne sheets and leave for a couple of minutes while you add the spinach to the tomato mixture and stir it in until it has wilted down.

When the spinach has wilted, add the lasagne sheets and mix it all together.

Plate up and add the pesto to each dish and serve.

DIETICIAN'S NOTES

Cooked tomatoes are a brilliant source of lycopene, a powerful antioxidant which helps keep our cells healthy. This dish would be ideal after a workout. To help your muscles recover, add more protein in the form of tofu, or up the quantity of lentils.

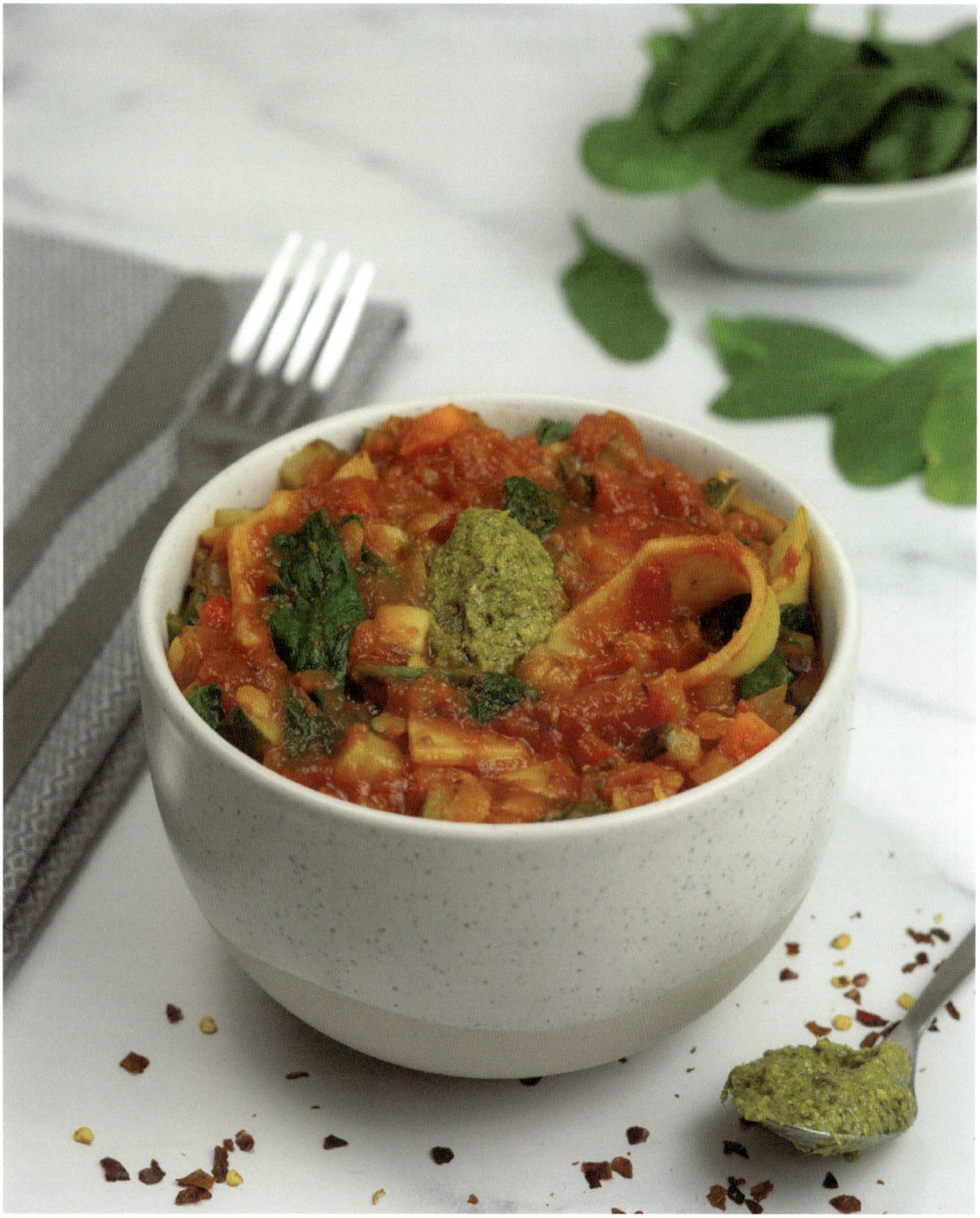

TOFU STIR FRY

(Per Serving) Calories 252 / Carbs 22g / Protein 14g / Fat 12g

This easy-to-make meal is packed with flavour - the hoisin and soy sauce compliments the tofu and vegetables really well. Serve over rice or on its own for a delicious weeknight meal.

Serves 2
Prep Time 10 mins
Cook Time 10 mins

INGREDIENTS

170g (6oz) Extra Firm Tofu 1/2 tsp Plain Flour
Pinch of Salt & Pepper 1 1/2 tbsp Olive Oil
2 tsps Maple Syrup
1tbsp Sesame Seeds 1 Garlic Clove (peeled and finely chopped)
A Thumb Sized Piece of Ginger (peeled and finely grated)
2 Spring Onion (thinly slices diagonally)
1 Red Chilli (thinly slices diagonally, leave seeds in for extra heat)
50g (1 3/4oz) Mangetout 1 Carrot (peeled and thinly sliced)
50g (1 3/4oz) Babycorn (cut each baby corn into small pieces)
70g (2 1/2oz) Tender Stem Broccoli (cut in half lengthways)
1 tbsp Light Soy Sauce 2 tbsp Hoisin Sauce

HOW TO COOK IT

Cut the tofu into roughly 1cm squares. Add to a large mixing bowl, sprinkle the plain flour over the tofu and season with salt and pepper. Mix so that the flour evenly covers the tofu.

Heat half the olive oil in a large frying pan over a medium heat, when hot add the tofu to the pan and cook for 4-5 minutes or until golden brown.

When cooked, place the tofu into a mixing bowl. Add the maple syrup and sesame seeds and mix it all together. Then put to one side until the vegetables are ready.

Add the remaining olive oil to a large deep frying pan or wok and heat to a medium heat.

Then add the garlic, ginger, spring onions and chilli. Stir them together and cook for about 2 minutes. Make sure the ingredients don't burn.

Then add the mangetout, carrot, baby corn and broccoli. Give them a quick stir and cook for about 5 minutes until the vegetables soften.

Add the soy sauce and hoisin sauce and stir the sauce into the vegetables

Add the tofu into the pan and stir one last time — Cook for 1 minute and then plate up.

DIETICIAN'S NOTES

Tofu is a great meat-free protein, which also contains calcium, vital for bone health. This low cal stir fry would make a tasty lunch or dinner - serve with rice for a more substantial meal, or for post-workout recovery.

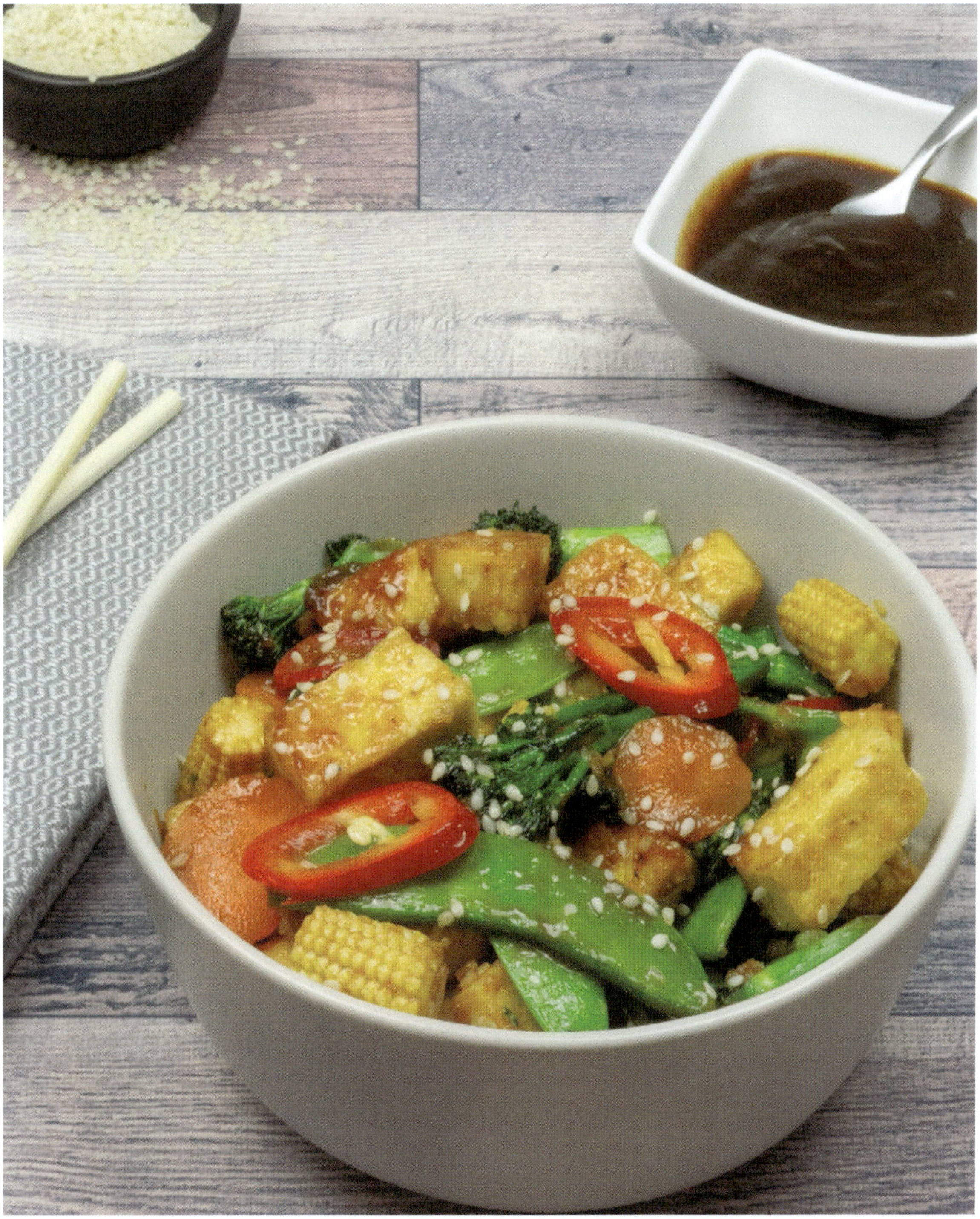

SWEET POTATO & WHITE BEAN CHILLI

(Per Serving) Calories 245 / Carbs 41g / Protein 9g / Fat 5g

This couourful meal combines warm spices with hearty root vegetables and is sure to leave you feeling full! Sweet potatoes work so well with the strong flavours of chilli. Replace kidney beans with white cannellini beans for a chilli with a twist.

| Serves 4
Prep Time 5 mins
Cook Time 45 mins

INGREDIENTS

400g (14oz) Sweet Potato (peeled, cut into 2cm slices widthways then cut into 4, see video)
2 tbsp Olive Oil
1tbsp Ground Cumin 1 tsp Smoked Paprika
2tsp Ground Cinnamon
½ Large Onion (finely chopped)
1 Red Chilli (fresh, deseeded and finely chopped)
2 Red Peppers (core removed and cut into squares)
1 Yellow Pepper (core removed and cut into squares)
1 Bunch of Fresh Coriander (Cilantro)
400g (14oz) Tin Cannellini Beans
400g (14oz) Tin of Chopped Tomatoes
2tsp Soya Plain Yogurt | ## HOW TO COOK IT

Preheat the oven to 180°C (350°F).

Place the sweet potato onto a baking tray. Add half of the olive oil. Sprinkle half of the cumin, paprika and cinnamon over the potato and mix it all together. Spread them out evenly over the baking tray and place in the oven for 35 minutes. They should be golden brown and soft when cooked.

In a large pan, heat the remaining olive oil over a medium heat.

Add the onion, chilli, peppers and roughly chopped coriander (cilantro) stems to the pan. Mix it all together.

Then add the remainder of the spices to the pan and mix well.

Turn the heat down to low and cook for 15 minutes, stirring occasionally.

Then add the cannellini beans, including the liquid, and the tinned tomatoes. Mix well and cook for 30 minutes, stirring occasionally.

Just before serving, add the sweet potato to the pan along with a small bunch of roughly chopped coriander (cilantro). Carefully mix it all together.

Plate up and add ½ tsp of soya plain yogurt to each dish and enjoy. |

DIETICIAN'S NOTES

Orange and yellow vegetables are a great source of vitamin A, which supports immune function. The beans and sweet potato are rich in fibre, which is important for digestive health. This dish will also score four of the recommended 5-A-DAY.

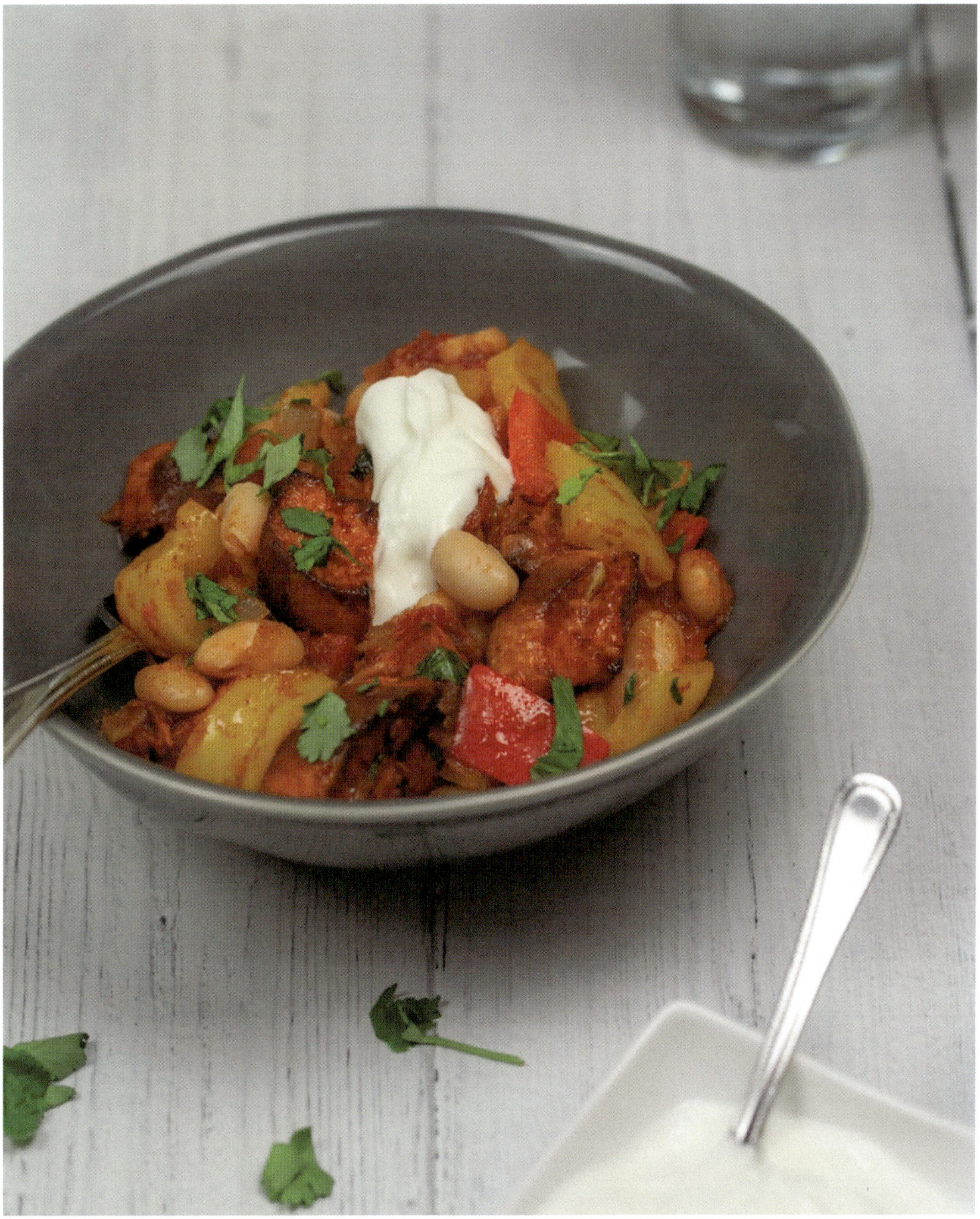

ROASTED CAULIFLOWER DHAL

(Per Serving) Calories 324 / Carbs 38g / Protein 16g / Fat 12g

Team golden roast cauliflower with curried lentils for a warming meat-free meal. Why not cook once eat twice by making a double batch of this curry? Leftovers freeze brilliantly.

Serves 4
Prep Time 6 mins
Cook Time 30 mins

INGREDIENTS

300g (10 1/2oz) Cauliflower (cut into bite size pieces)
3 tbsp Olive Oil
Pinch of Salt & Pepper 1 Brown Onion (finely chopped)
3 Garlic Cloves (finely chopped)
1 tbsp Mustard Seeds 1 tsp Cumin
1 Thumb Sized Piece of Ginger (peeled & grated)
400g (14oz) Chopped Tomatoes
250g (8 3/4oz) Red Split Lentils
500ml (2 cups) Water
Bunch Fresh Coriander (cilantro) (roughly chopped)
2tsp Soya Yogurt

HOW TO COOK IT

Preheat the oven to 200°C (390°F).

Add the cauliflower to a mixing bowl. Add 2 tbsp of olive oil, season with a pinch of salt and pepper, then place the cauliflower onto a non-stick baking tray in a single layer and cook in the oven for 15-20 minutes until golden brown. Once cooked, put to one side.

Heat the remainder of the oil in a large, deep non-stick pan over a low-medium heat.

Add the onion and cook for 3-4 minutes.

Then add the garlic and cook for a further 2 minutes.

Add the mustard seeds, cumin and ginger. Cook for 2 minutes before adding the chopped tomatoes. Stir well before adding the lentils and 500ml of water.

Bring the pan to a simmer and then reduce the heat and cook for 20-25 minutes, stirring occasionally. When done, the lentils should be beginning to break down.

Season well with salt and pepper.

Add in the cooked cauliflower and half of the coriander (cilantro) and gently stir. Trying to keep the cauliflower pieces whole.

Plate up the cauliflower dhal and top with the soya yogurt and a sprinkle of coriander (cilantro).

DIETICIAN'S NOTES

This is a balanced dish containing carbs, protein and heart-healthy fats from olive oil. The protein and fibre in the lentils will make this a filling meal - add extra soya yogurt for more of a protein boost. If this is a post-workout meal, team with rice

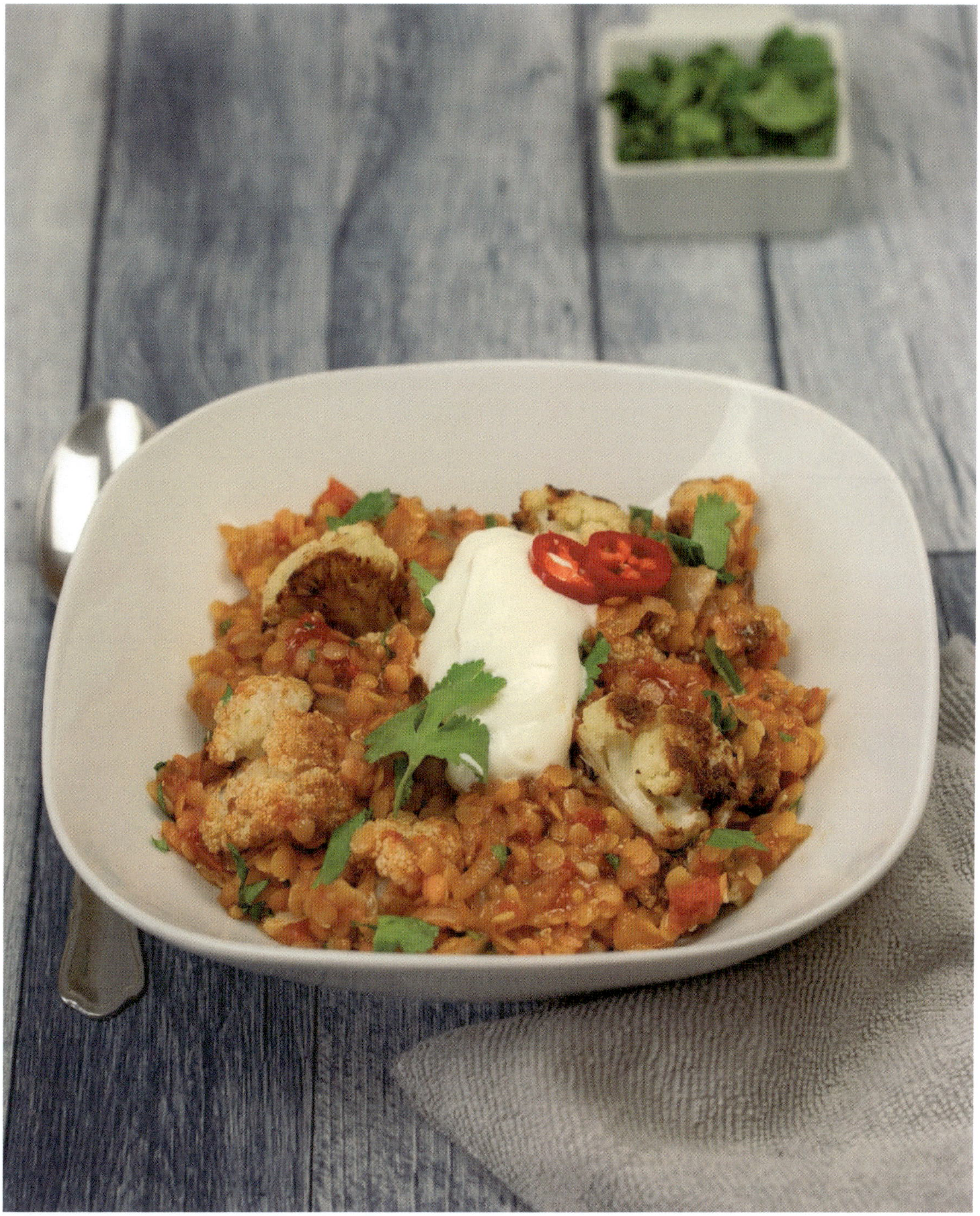

VEGETABLE RED THAI CURRY

(Per Serving) Calories 352 / Carbs 45g / Protein 7g / Fat 16g

This is an excellent dish for entertaining and having friends round, it's a real crowd-pleaser! Ready in just thirty minutes, this fragrant Thai curry is sure to tantalise your taste buds with salty, spicy, sour and sweet flavours!

Serves 2
Prep Time 5 mins
Cook Time 30 mins

INGREDIENTS

1 tbsp Olive Oil
1/2 Red Onion (peeled and finely chopped)
1 Garlic Clove (peeled and finely chopped)
1/2 Red Chilli (deseeded and finely chopped)
25g (1oz) Red Thai Curry Paste
200ml (3/4cup) Light Coconut Milk
125ml (1/2cup) Water
250g (8 3/4oz) Sweet Potato (cut into chunks)
100g (3 1/2oz) Green Beans (ends trimmed and cut in half)
1/2 Tin (200g / 7oz) (non-drained weight) Chickpeas (drained and rinsed)
1/2 Lime (cut into wedges)

HOW TO COOK IT

Add the oil to a large non-stick pan and heat to a medium heat. Add the onion, cook for 3-4 minutes until they start to brown. Then add the garlic and chilli and cook for 30 seconds.

Then add the red Thai paste, coconut milk and water to the pan. Give it a quick stir. Turn the heat up and bring to the boil before adding the sweet potato. Reduce to a medium heat and simmer for 12-15 minutes.

Add the green beans and chickpeas and cook for a further 5-10 minutes. Divide the curry into 2 dishes and serve.
Squeeze in the lime for extra flavour.

OPTIONAL: If you want more carbohydrates, you can add rice to this dish. Just scan the rice in separately if tracking calories.

NOTE: If the sweet potato is still too crunchy, cut it up a little smaller next time.

DIETICIAN'S NOTES

Spices like chilli and garlic have powerful antioxidant properties, which help keep cells healthy. To increase the protein content, add some cubed tofu to the curry.

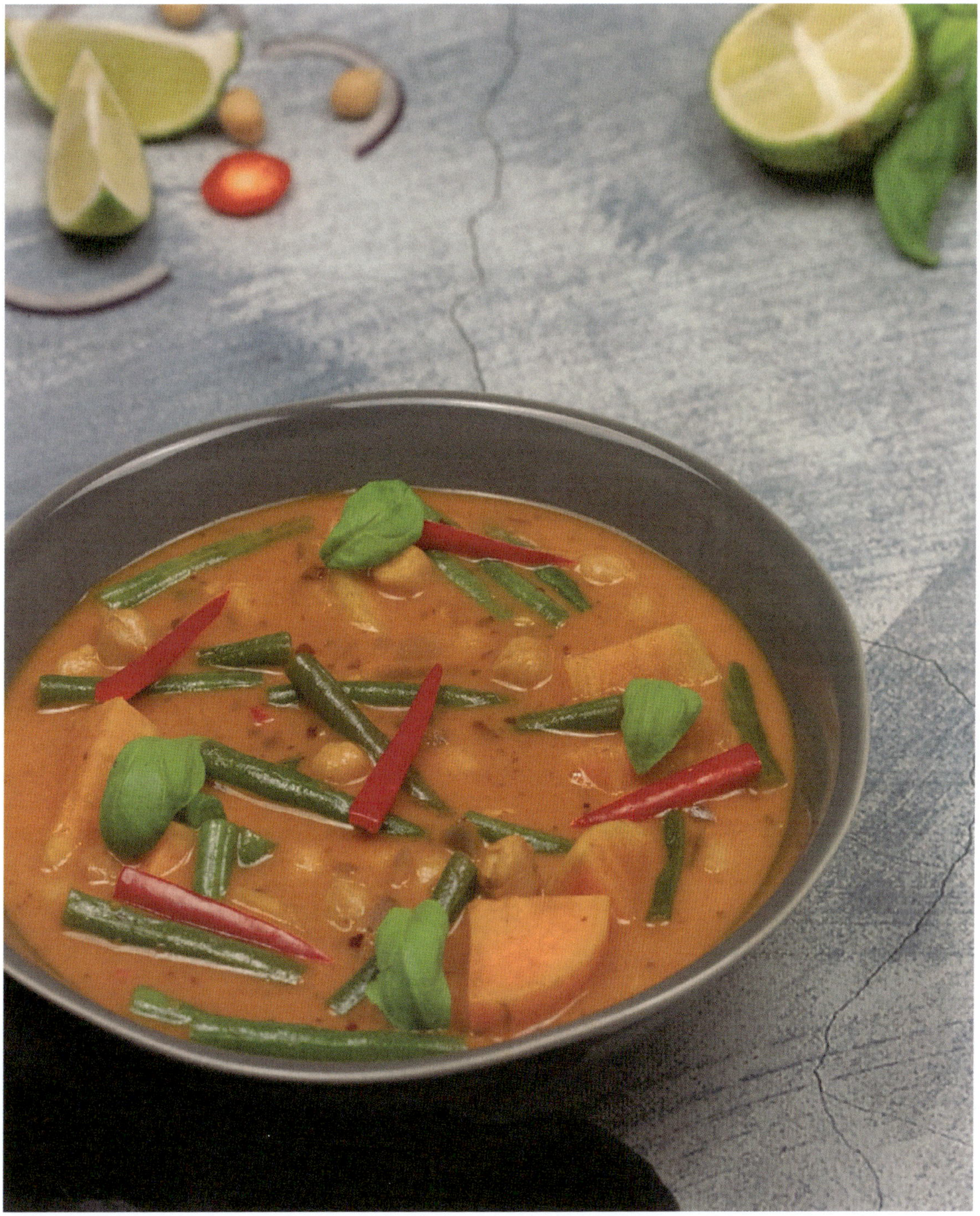

BBQ CHICKPEA & WALNUT BURGER

(Per Serving) Calories 531 / Carbs 63g / Protein 18g / Fat 23g

These delicious vegan burgers are chock-full of nutritious ingredients and jam-packed with big flavours, including soy, hoisin, mustard and garlic. Whip up a big batch and freeze for during the week, or if you're having friends around. Add vegan BBQ sauce and salad and you've got a sure-fire hit.

Serves 2 Prep Time 10 mins Cook Time 10 mins ## INGREDIENTS 25g (3/4oz) Couscous (uncooked weight) 40ml Boiling Water 40g (1 1/2oz) Walnuts 80g (2 3/4oz) Chickpeas (canned, drained well) 1/2 tbsp Soy Sauce 1 tbsp Tomato Paste 1/2 tbsp Vegan Mayonnaise 1 tsp Hoisin Sauce 1/2 tsp Dijon Mustard Pinch Garlic Powder 1/2 tsp Smoked Paprika Pinch of Salt & Pepper 15g (1/2oz) Plain Flour 1 Tbsp Olive Oil 1 1/2 Tbsp Vegan Barbecue Sauce 2 Hamburger Buns 4 Lettuce Leaves (washed) 1 Beef Tomato (sliced) 1/2 Red Onion (sliced)	## HOW TO COOK IT Add the couscous to a small mixing bowl. Pour over the boiling water, cover with a tea towel and leave to stand for 10 minutes. Add the walnuts to a blender and blend. Once done, put to one side. Add the chickpeas, soy sauce and tomato paste to a food processor and blend. You may need to stop a couple of times and scoop the mixture off the sides. Once mixed, add the chickpea mixture to a large mixing bowl. Add the following ingredients to the chickpea mixture: blended walnuts, vegan mayonnaise, hoisin sauce, Dijon mustard, garlic powder, smoked paprika, salt and pepper. Give it a quick stir, before adding the couscous and plain flour. Get your hands in there and give it a really good mix. Split the mixture into 2 balls and then shape them into burgers. Heat a large frying pan to a medium heat, add the olive oil and when hot add the burgers to the pan. Brush the top of each burger with some of the barbecue sauce and cook for 5 minutes. Flip the burgers and brush on a little more barbecue sauce and cook for a further 5 minutes. While the burgers are cooking, prepare the buns, lettuce, tomatoe and red onion. Tower up your burger and finish off with a little barbecue sauce on top of each burger. Serve up and enjoy.

DIETICIAN'S NOTES

A great way to enjoy a burger with some vegetable benefits! The fats from the nuts and olive oil are heart-healthy, and then chickpeas add fibre. Choose a seeded wholegrain bun to score extra nutrients.

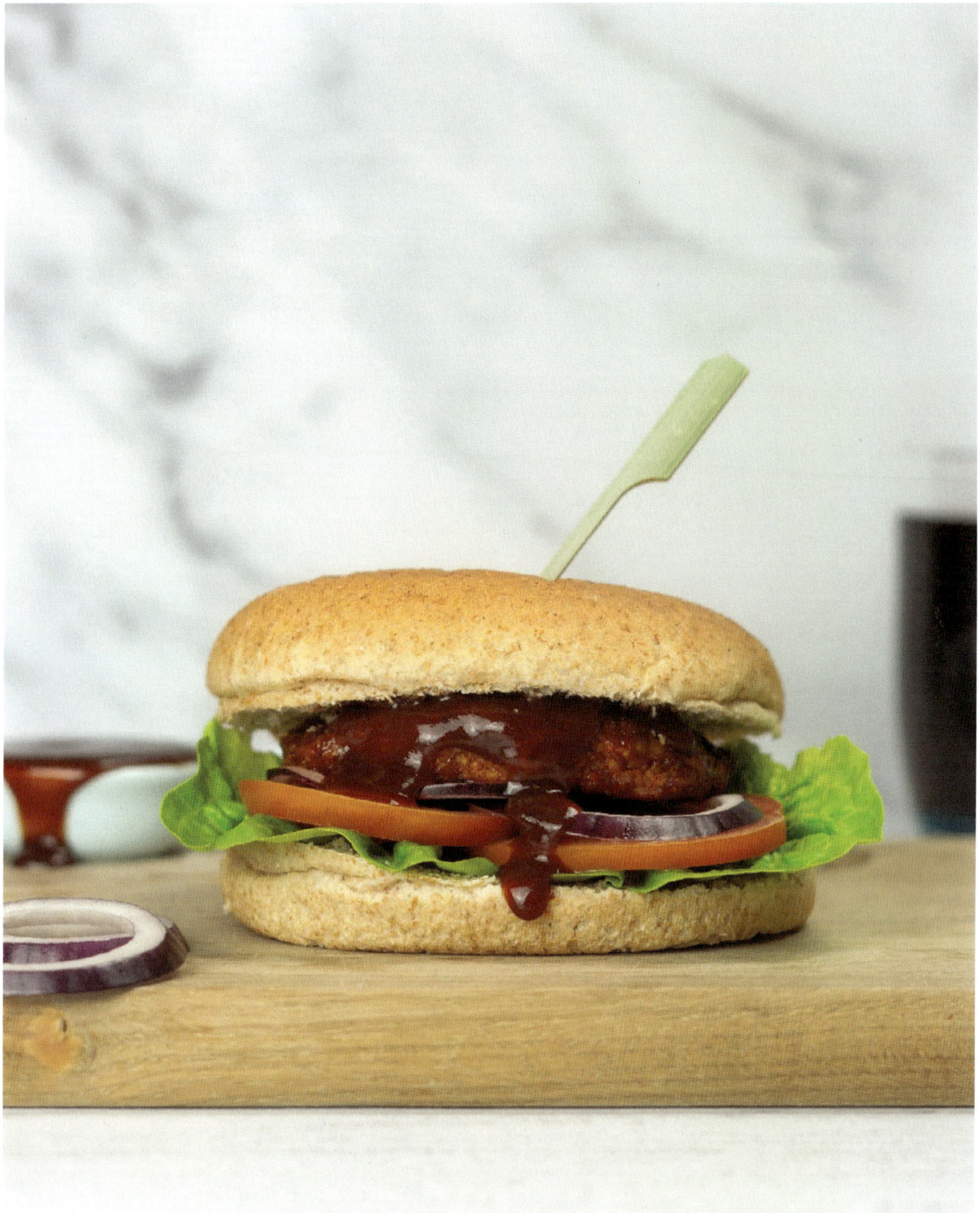

CHICKPEA & RED SPLIT LENTIL CURRY

(Per Serving) Calories 365 / Carbs 42g / Protein 20g / Fat 13g

Takeaways can top 1000 calories a meal.... but this quick, super-healthy curry is a great alternative. It's full of flavour and won't bust your calorie budget. Serve with your choice of steamed rice.

Serves 4
Prep Time 5 mins
Cook Time 35 mins

INGREDIENTS

1 tbsp Olive Oil
1 Small Onion (finely chopped)
2 Garlic Cloves (finely chopped)
1 1/2 tbsp Mild Curry Powder
1/2 tsp Cumin
1/2 tsp Paprika
Pinch of Salt
400g (14oz) Tomato Passata
400g (14oz) Reduced Fat Coconut Milk
400g (14oz) Canned Chickpeas (drained and rinsed)
50g (1 3/4oz) Red Split Lentils
250g (8 3/4oz) Meat Free Chicken Pieces
250g (8 3/4oz) Wholegrain Microwavable Rice
Red Chilli (for garnishing)
Coriander (cilantro) (for garnishing)
1 Lime (cut in wedges)

HOW TO COOK IT

Heat half of the olive oil in a large non-stick pan over a medium heat.

Then add the onion and cook for 4 minutes, if it starts to burn, turn the heat down.

Then add the garlic and cook for 30 seconds.

Now add the curry powder, cumin and paprika. Give it a quick stir, so the onion and garlic are covered in the spices.

Add the salt, passata, coconut milk, chickpeas and lentils. Mix it all together. Turn the heat up until the sauce is bubbling then reduce the heat to medium/low and simmer for 10 minutes.

Meanwhile, add the remaining olive oil to a large frying pan over a medium/high heat. When hot, add in the frozen meat-free chicken pieces and cook for 10 minutes until they are slightly brown. Then add them to the curry mixture.

Stir the meat-free chicken pieces into the curry and let the curry simmer for 20 minutes. The sauce should be nice and thick when the curry is ready. Note: If you find the curry is getting too dry, you can always add a few tablespoons of water to loosen the sauce.

Prepare the rice in the microwave.

Plate up the rice with the curry and finish with a few slices of chopped chilli (if you like it hot) a garnish of coriander and a wedge of lime.

DIETICIAN'S NOTES

Containing some fab sources of vegan protein, this is a well balanced, filling dish. Chickpeas are a great source of gut-friendly fibre, and the spices are packed with antioxidants.

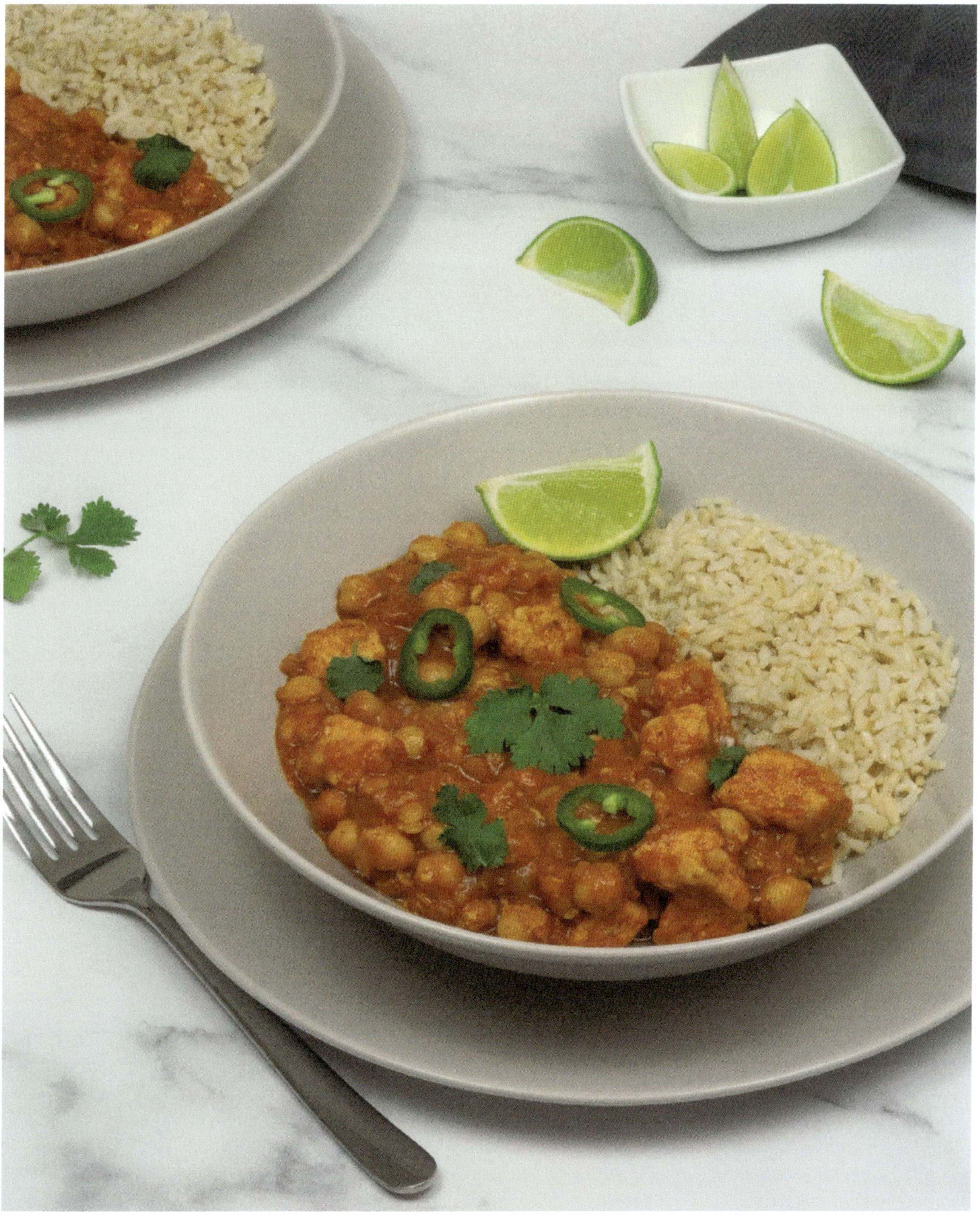

SAAG ALOO

(Per Serving) Calories 155 / Carbs 27g / Protein 5g / Fat 3g

A regular on most Indian menus, this tasty potato and spinach based dish is great as a main meal or side dish. You can make your own spice mix for this or use curry powder. Pack in spinach for extra nutrients!

Serves 4
Prep Time 5 mins
Cook Time 20 mins

INGREDIENTS

1 tbsp Olive Oil
1 Brown Onion (finely chopped)
20g (3/4oz) Ginger (peeled and grated)
2 Garlic Cloves (finely chopped)
3/4 tsp Ground Coriander (Cilantro)
3/4 tsp Ground Cumin
½ tsp Ground Turmeric
1/2 Vegetable Stock Cube
300ml (1 1/4cups) Boiling Water
400g (14oz) White Potatoes (cut into chunks)
1 Large Tomato (cut into chunks)
Pinch of Salt
Pinch of Pepper
200g (7oz) Baby Spinach (washed)
1/2 Lime (juice)
4 tsp Soya Yogurt
Coriander (Cilantro) (for garnishing)
1 Green Chilli (thinly sliced)

HOW TO COOK IT

Heat the olive oil in a large deep non-stick frying pan on a medium heat.

Add the onion and cook for 4-5 minutes until it starts to brown. Then add the ginger, garlic, ground coriander (cilantro), ground cumin and ground turmeric to the pan and stir it all together.

Add the stock cube to boiling water and allow it to dissolve.

Add the potatoes to the pan and cover the potatoes in the spiced onion mixture.

Now add the tomato, vegetable stock and a pinch of salt and pepper to the pan. Give it all a good stir. Increase the heat to high. Bring to the boil and then reduce to a medium heat and simmer for 12 minutes.

If the sauce gets too dry, add a few tablespoons of water to loosen it.

Check the potatoes with a shape knife. If the potato falls off the blade, then they are ready.

Add the spinach to the pan and cover the pan until the spinach has wilted. This should only take a couple of minutes.

Then, stir the spinach into the dish. Do it gently; otherwise, you may break up the potatoes.

Add the lime juice. Plate up, add the soya yogurt to each dish and garnish with coriander (cilantro) leaves and green chillis (these will give the recipe a little heat).

DIETICIAN'S NOTES

Potatoes are a good source of vitamin C, which supports immune function and healthy skin. This is a low-calorie dish - perfect as a side or team with some rice for a more substantial main meal. You could also top with extra soya yogurt to increase the protein content.

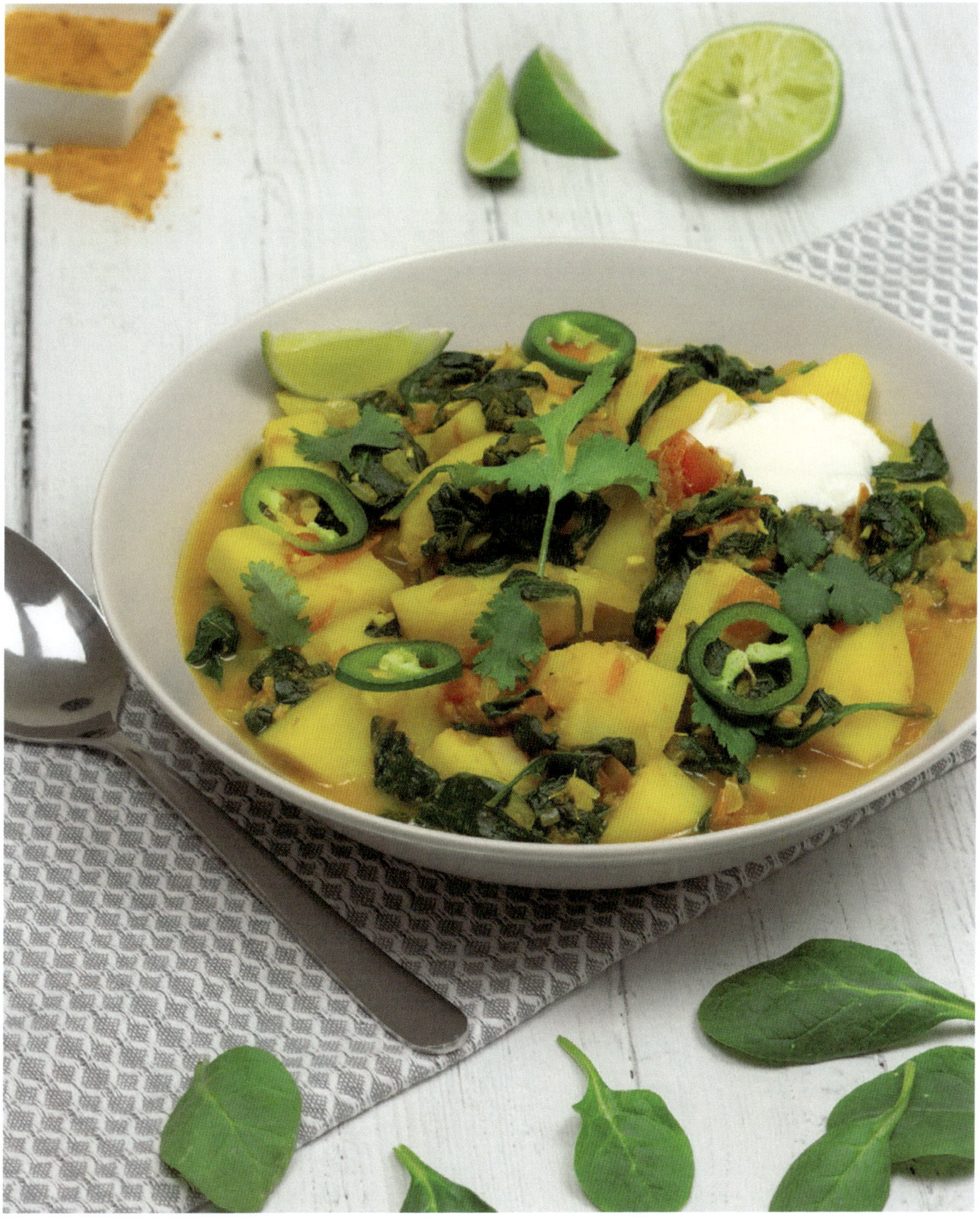

RED SPLIT LENTIL DAHL

(Per Serving) Calories 296 / Carbs 34g / Protein 13g / Fat 12g

This quick-to-make flavourful vegan dahl is perfect comfort food. It's also freezer friendly, so make the most of your time by batch cooking and freezing the extra portions.

Serves 2
Prep Time 5 mins
Cook Time 25 mins

INGREDIENTS

1 tbsp Olive Oil
1/2 Brown Onion (finely chopped)
1 tbsp Ginger (peeled and finely grated)
2 Garlic Cloves (finely chopped)
1 tsp Green Chilli (finely chopped, including seeds)
1/2 tsp Ground Cumin
1/2 tsp Ground Coriander (Cilantro)
1/2 tsp Garam Masala
1/4 tsp Turmeric
1/4 Vegetable Stock Cube
150ml (3/4cup) Boiling Water
135g (4 3/4oz) Red Split Lentils (rinsed)
200g (7oz) Chopped Tomatoes (either fresh or tinned)
200ml (1 cup) Light Coconut Milk
Pinch of Salt & Pepper
Fresh Coriander (Cilantro) (for garnish)

HOW TO COOK IT

Add the olive oil to a large deep frying pan and heat to a medium heat.

Then add the onion and cook for about 3 minutes. Don't let the onion burn.

Then add the ginger, garlic and green chilli, give it a quick stir and cook for 30 seconds.

Then add the cumin, coriander, garam masala and turmeric. Mix the spices with the onion mixture.

Dissolve the vegetable stock cube in boiling water. While this is dissolving, add in the lentils, chopped tomatoes, coconut milk, dissolved vegetable stock, salt and pepper. Give it a quick stir, increase the heat and bring to the boil.

When bubbling, reduced the heat to a low-medium heat and place a lid over the pan and cook for around 20 minutes or until your desired texture. If the lentils are still a little tough, add a drop more water and cook for a few more minutes (see the video for ideal texture).

Plate up and top with a few extra chillis for heat and coriander (cilantro).

DIETICIAN'S NOTES

Split lentils are super easy to cook, and make a helpful meat substitute thanks to their protein content. They're also a super source of fibre, which helps to feed the helpful bacteria in your gut.

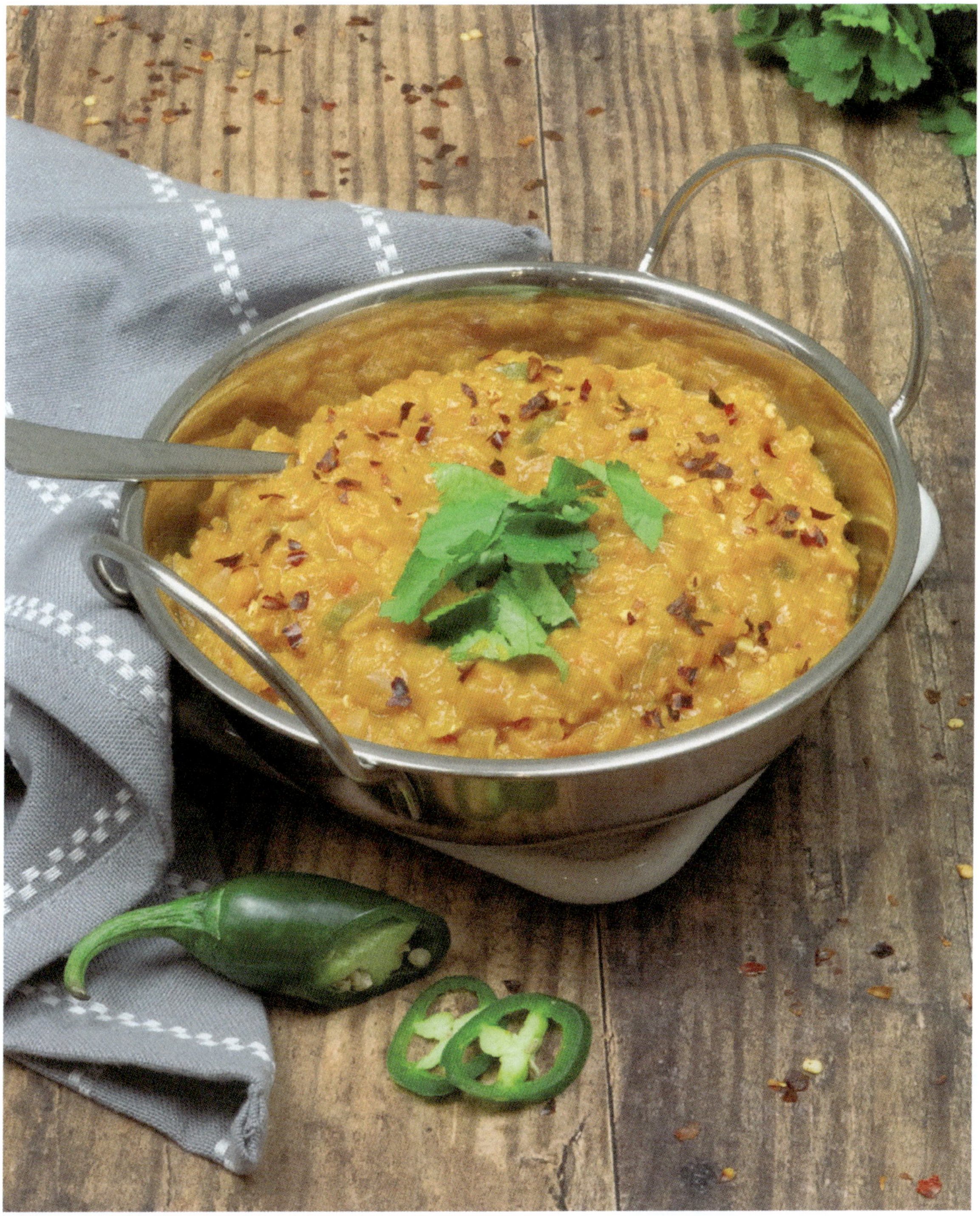

VEGAN SOYA CHILLI

(Per Serving) Calories 372 / Carbs 44g / Protein 22g / Fat 12g

This vegan chilli is an easy vegan mid-week dinner and packs a real flavour punch! Full of plant-based protein (like kidney beans), it features soya mince, fibre-rich lentils and vitamin-packed avocados.

Serves 4
Prep Time 10 mins
Cook Time 30 mins

INGREDIENTS

1 tbsp Olive Oil
1/2 Red Onion
(finely chopped)
2 Garlic Cloves
(finely chopped)
70g (2 1/2oz) Red Bell Peppers
(thinly chopped)
1 Medium Carrot
(peeled and thinly chopped)
1 Celery Sticks
(thinly chopped)
1/2 tsp Cumin
1/2 tsp Chilli Powder Pinch of Salt & Pepper
1/2 Vegetable Stock Cube
170ml (3/4 cup) Boiling Water 600g (21oz) Chopped Tomatoes
1 x 400g (14oz) Tin Kidney Beans
(drained & washed)
250g (8 3/4oz) Soya Mince 60g (2oz) Red Split Lentils
(uncooked weight)
1 tbsp Balsamic Vinegar
A Bunch of Coriander (cilantro) 250g (8 3/4oz) Microwavable Rice 1 Avocado
(stone & skin removed & cut into chunks)
1 Red Chilli
(thinly sliced)

HOW TO COOK IT

Add the olive oil to a large non-stick pan over a medium heat.

Add the red onion, garlic, red bell peppers, carrot and celery — Cook for about 4 minutes.

Then add the cumin, chilli powder, salt and pepper and mix well. Dissolve the vegetable stock cube in the boiling water.

Now add the chopped tomatoes, kidney beans, soya mince, red split lentils, vegetable stock and balsamic vinegar, stir well and bring the pan to the boil.

Once simmering, reduce the heat to medium and cook for 25 minutes. If the liquid starts to dry, add a little extra water.

When the dish is almost ready, add in some of the coriander and give it a quick stir.

Prepare the rice.

Split the rice and the chilli into 4 bowls and finish by adding the avocado, coriander and a few slices of chilli

DIETICIAN'S NOTES

A nicely balanced dish containing a good proportion of carbohydrates, protein and heart-healthy fats from avocado and olive oil. This meal should keep your energy levels on an even keel and hunger at bay.

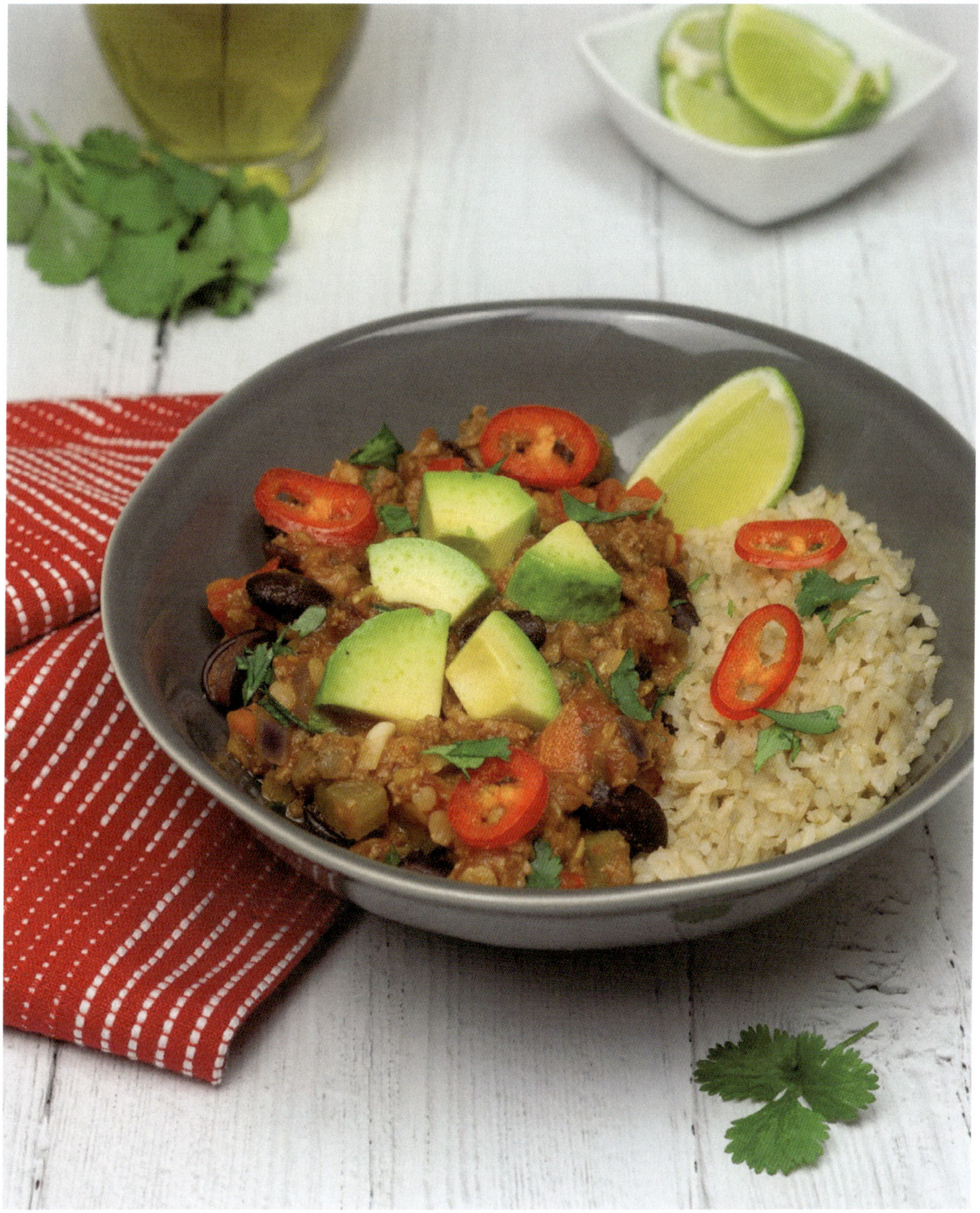

LENTIL PIE

(Per Serving) Calories 239 / Carbs 42g / Protein 11g / Fat 3g

This delicious lentil pie is the ultimate comfort food and is perfect for a hearty dinner or weekend lunch. Make it in bulk and freeze it into separate servings to save time during the week. Serve with broccoli to score one more of your 5-A-DAY.

Serves 4
Prep Time 10 mins
Cook Time 40 mins

INGREDIENTS

400g (14oz) Potato (peeled and roughly chopped) 40ml (dash) Non-Dairy Milk Pinch of Salt & Pepper
1 tbsp Olive Oil
½ Vegetable Stock Cube 240ml (1cup) Boiling Water 1 Medium Onion (peeled and finely chopped)
3 Garlic Cloves (peeled and finely chopped)
1 Large Carrot (peeled, quartered lengthways and thinly sliced)
1 Celery Stick (quartered lengthways and thinly sliced)
240g (8 1/2oz) Passata 1 tsp Rosemary
1 tsp Thyme
1 tbsp Light Soy Sauce
1 tbsp Worcestershire Sauce
190g (6 3/4oz) Tinned Cooked Lentils in Water (drained)
2 tbsp Cornstarch
2 tbsp Water
300g (10 1/2oz) Tenderstem Broccoli

HOW TO COOK IT

Preheat the oven to 200°C (390°F).

Boil the kettle. Once boiled, add the water to a large saucepan. Add the potatoes and simmer for 12-15 minutes. Check if the potatoes are cooked with the blade of a shape knife. If the potatoes fall off the blade, then they are ready.

Drain the potatoes, add the non-dairy milk and mash until the potato is nice and smooth. You can add a little salt for flavour if you want. Put to one side for later.

While the potatoes are cooking, heat the olive oil in a large deep non-stick frying pan on a medium heat.

Add the stock cube to the boiling water and allow it to dissolve.

Now, add the onion, garlic, carrot and celery to the non-stick pan a cook for about 5 minutes. Don't allow the garlic and onion to burn.

Pour the vegetable stock and passata into the pan along with the rosemary, thyme, soy sauce, Worcestershire sauce, salt and pepper. Stir it and simmer for 10 minutes.

Then add in the lentils and allow to warm to 2 minutes.

Add a couple to tablespoons of water to the cornstarch and mix it together before adding it the pan and stirring it through. Cook for a few more minutes to allow the sauce to thicken.

When the sauce has thickened, add the lentil mixture to a non-stick ovenproof dish. Top it with the mash. Use a fork to rough up the top of the mashed potato and then place in the oven and cook for 20minutes.

Add the broccoli to boiling water and cook for roughly 4 minutes or to your preferred texture.

Plate up and enjoy.

DIETICIAN'S NOTES

Pulses like lentils are a great contributor to protein in a vegan diet, plus they boast high levels of fibre, which support digestive health. This is a low cal dish, so consider serving a larger portion if you're eating this after a workout, to provide the right mix of nutrients for recovery.

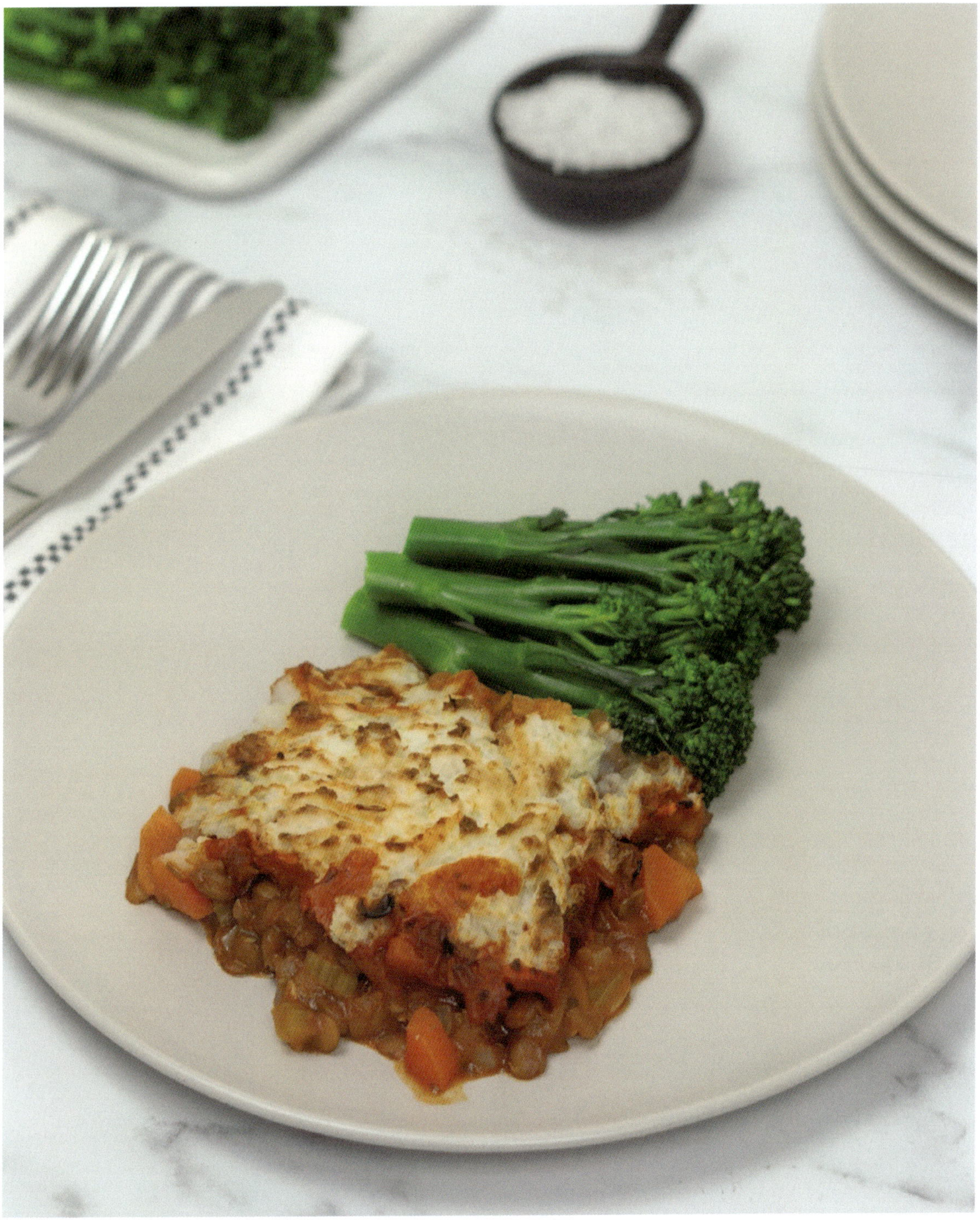

BUTTERNUT SQUASH RISOTTO

(Per Serving) Calories 294 / Carbs 53g / Protein 7g / Fat 6g

With its creamy texture and earthy flavour, this comforting vegan dinner feels like a big, warm hug! Fibre-packed squash goes well with peas in this satisfying risotto. Make more than you need for tasty leftovers!

Serves 4 Prep Time 5 mins Cook Time 30 mins ## INGREDIENTS 400g (14oz) Butternut Squash (peeled, deseeded and cut into cubes) 2 tsp Olive Oil Pinch of Salt Pinch of Pepper 1 Vegetable Stock Cube 800ml (3 1/4cups) Boiling Water 1/2 Large Brown Onion (peeled and finely chopped) 1 Garlic Clove (peeled and finely chopped) 200g (7oz) Arborio Risotto Rice 1/2 tbsp Dried Sage 120g (4 1/4oz) Frozen Peas 1 tsp Unsalted Vegetable Spread	## HOW TO COOK IT Preheat the oven to 220°C (430°F). Add the butternut squash to a non-stick baking tray. Pour over half of the olive oil, season with salt and pepper and place in the oven for 30 minutes until golden brown. In a large saucepan, dilute the vegetable stock cube in the boiling water and keep on the hob over a low heat to ensure it stays hot. Heat the remaining olive oil in a large non-stick pan over a medium heat. Add the onion and cook for 3 minutes. Add the garlic and cook for 30 seconds. Add the Arborio Risotto Rice and sage, give it a quick stir. Add in 1 ladle of the hot vegetable stock to the rice and stir it in. When the rice has absorbed the liquid, add another ladle of vegetable stock. Keep doing this until the rice has absorbed all the liquid. It should take 15-20 minutes. When the rice has absorbed nearly all the liquid, add the frozen peas and vegetable spread. Stir and cook for a further 2 minutes. Remove the rice from the heat, add the cooked butternut squash and mix it in. Put a lid over the rice and leave to stand for 2 minutes. Plate up and enjoy.

DIETICIAN'S NOTES

Higher carbohydrate meals like this dish are great after a workout, as they help your muscles to replenish their glycogen (energy) stores. Try topping with nutritional yeast for added B vitamins including B12, which is only naturally present in animal foods.

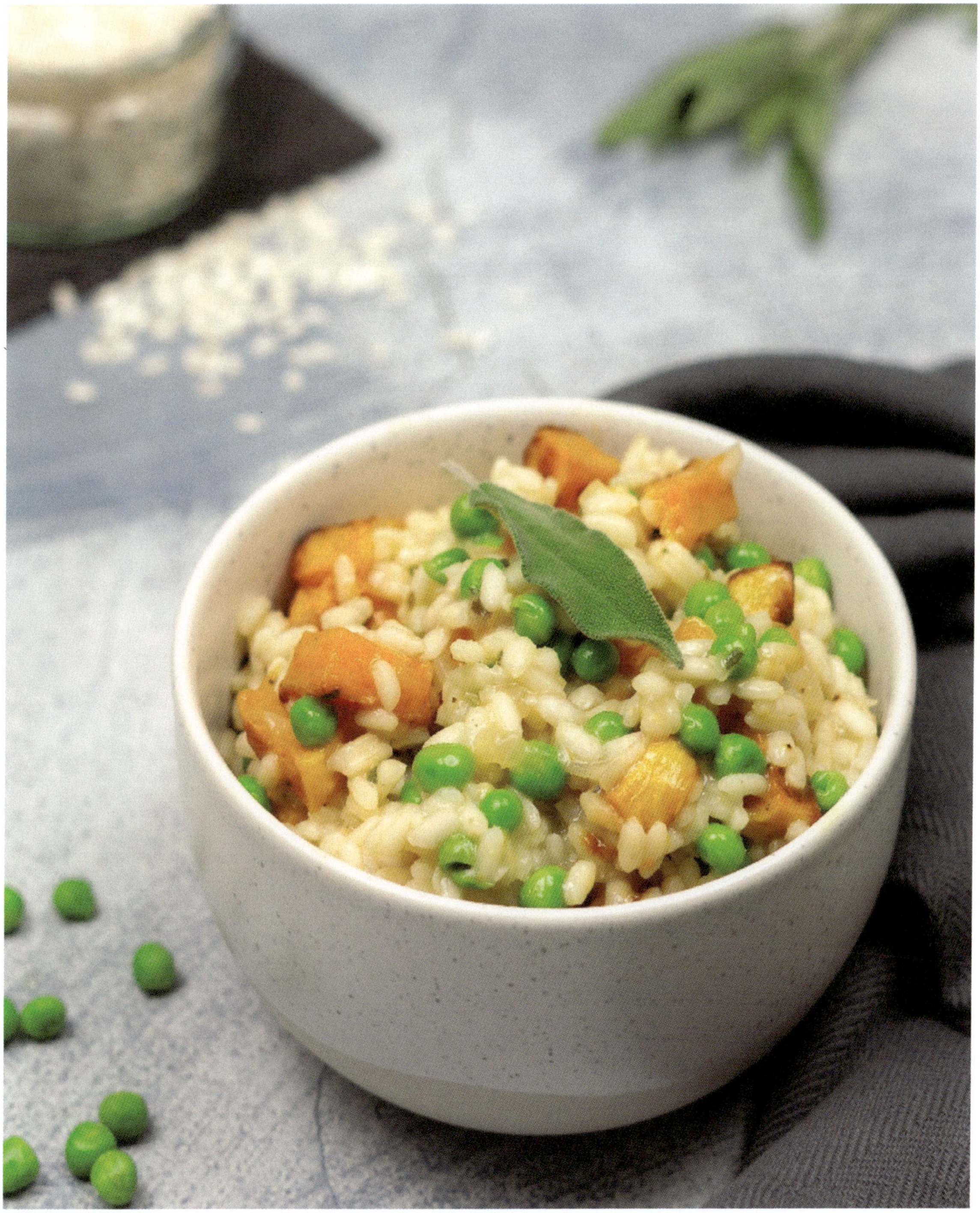

ONE POT CHILLI THAI PASTA

(Per Serving) Calories 375 / Carbs 56g / Protein 13g / Fat 11g

Quick to make, this one-pot pasta is packed with fresh, nutritious vegetables (tomatoes, peppers, courgette). Red Thai paste and chilli add spicy and sweet flavours. If you've never tried red Thai paste with pasta, then you're missing out!

Serves 2
Prep Time 7 mins
Cook Time 20 mins

INGREDIENTS

3/4 tbsp Olive Oil
1/2 Brown Onion (finely chopped)
100g (3 1/2oz) Red Bell Peppers (cut in small chunks)
125g (4 1/2oz) Courgette (cut in small chunks)
2 Garlic Cloves (finely chopped)
50g (1 3/4oz) Petit Pois
Thumb Sized Piece of Ginger (peeled and finely chopped)
1 Red Chilli (finely chopped, add the seeds for extra heat)
100g (3 1/2oz) Fusilli Wholegrain Pasta
400g (14oz) Tinned Chopped Tomatoes
100ml (1/2cup) Coconut Milk (reduced fat)
1 tsp Red Thai Paste 1/2 Lemon (Juiced) Pinch of Salt & Pepper
100g (3 1/2oz) Cherry Tomatoes

HOW TO COOK IT

Add the olive to a large deep frying pan and heat to a medium heat.

Add the onion and cook for 3 minutes. Then add in the red bell pepper, courgette and garlic and cook for 2 more minutes.

Add the remaining ingredients (apart from the cherry tomatoes) give it a quick stir and bring to a simmer. Cook for 12 minutes, stirring occasionally.

Then add the cherry tomatoes, stir and cook for a further 3 minutes. Plate up and enjoy.

Note: This dish is great for bulk cooking.

DIETICIAN'S NOTES

A vegetable packed pasta dish with plenty of vitamin C. Choosing wholegrain pasta is a great way to boost your fibre intake, helping you stay fuller for longer.

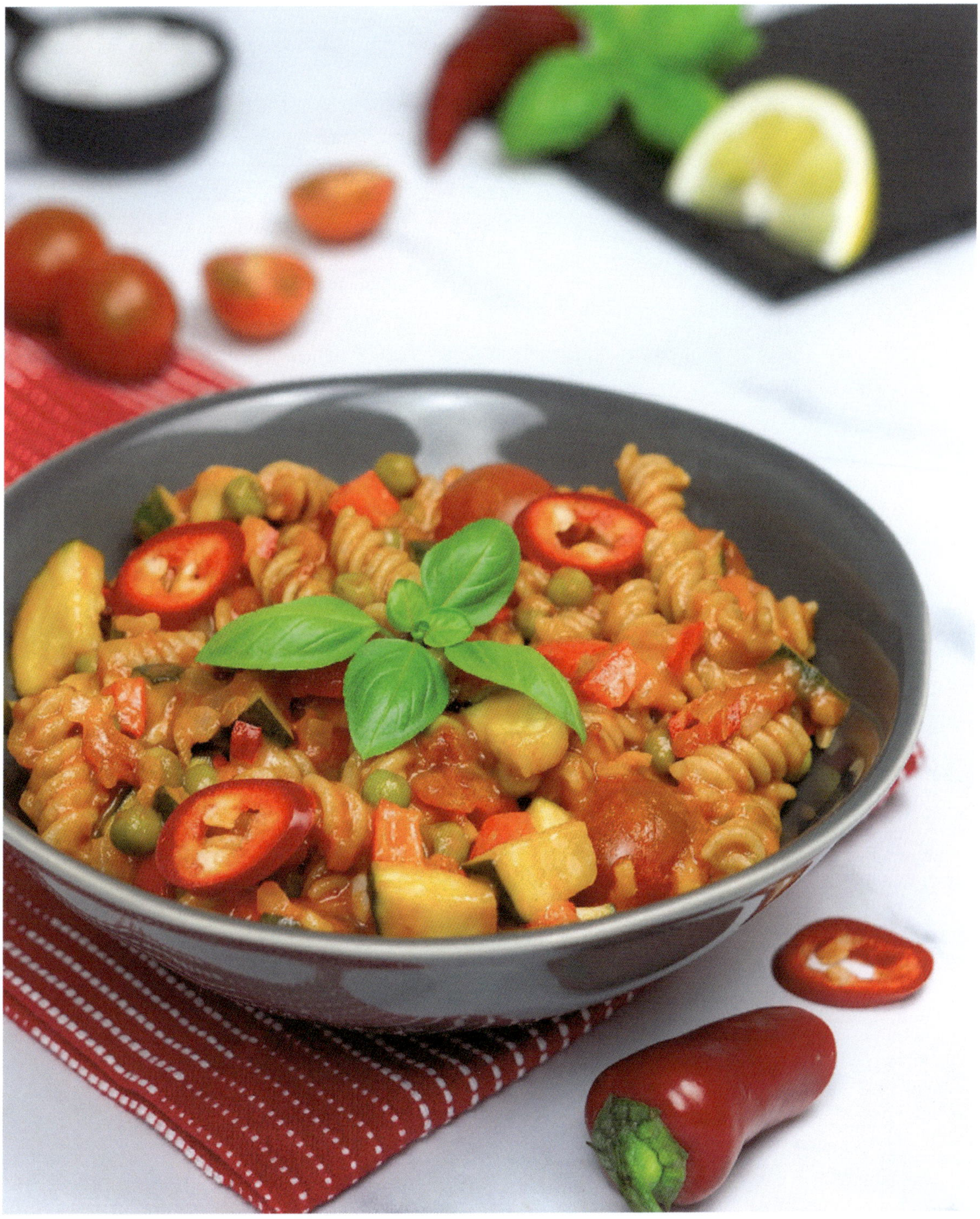

VEGETABLE CRISPS

(Per Serving) Calories 109 / Carbs 14g / Protein 2g / Fat 5g

Satisfy your crisp cravings with this healthy alternative which take just minutes to prepare, then let the oven do the rest! Carrot, sweet potato and beetroot slices create a delicious snack (make sure that they are wafer- thin for crispiness).

Serves 2
Prep Time 10 mins
Cook Time 20 mins

INGREDIENTS

100g (3 1/2oz) Carrot (peeled and finely sliced)
100g (3 1/2oz) Sweet Potato (peeled and finely sliced)
1 tbsp Olive Oil
Pinch of Salt & Pepper
1 tsp Paprika or Cayenne Pepper
50g (1 3/4oz) Beetroot (peeled and finely sliced)

HOW TO COOK IT

Preheat the oven to 170°C (340°F).

Make sure the vegetables are cut to a wafer-thin thickness. Otherwise, they won't crisp up in the oven.

Add the carrot and sweet potato to a large mixing bowl.

Then add 3/4 tbsp of olive oil to the mixing bowl, as well as salt, pepper and your chosen seasoning (paprika or cayenne pepper). Mix it all together and add to a non-stick baking sheet. Alternatively, add to an oven proof tray lined with a baking sheet. Make sure they are placed on the baking tray in a single layer. If they are overlapping, they won't crisp up.

Repeat the process with the beetroot but with only 1/4 tbsp olive oil and a small sprinkle of your chosen seasoning. Give it a quick mix.

Place both trays into the oven and cook for about 20 minutes, turning them halfway through cooking.

Keep a close eye on them. They will all cook at a different speed depending on the thickness. Some may require less or more time. They are cooked when they turn golden brown.

Once cooked allow to stand for 10 minutes to crisp up before serving

DIETICIAN'S NOTES

Oven baking means these veggie crisps stay lower in fat making them a great alternative to regular crisps.

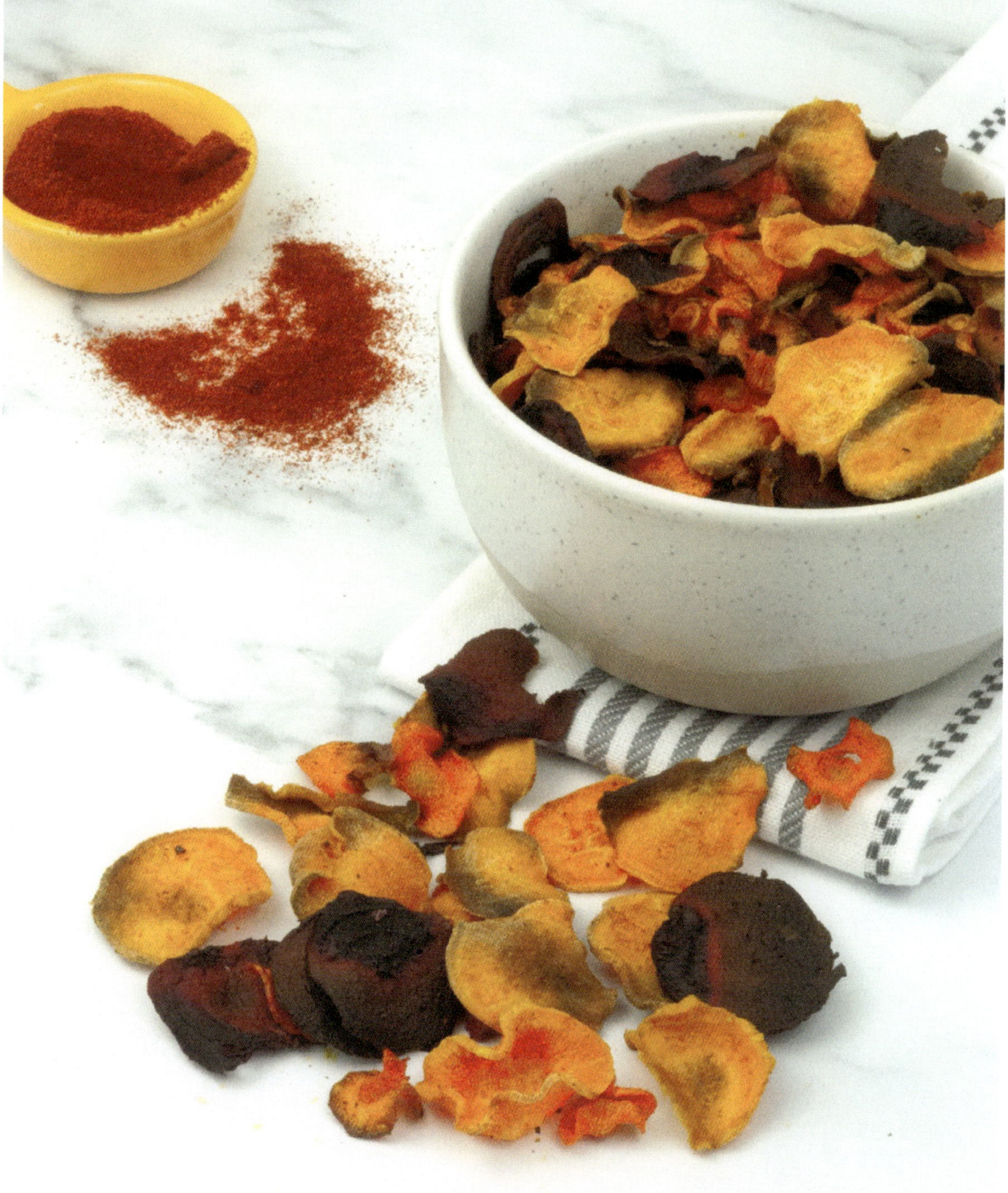

DATE BOATS

(Per Serving) Calories 109 / Carbs 14g / Protein 2g / Fat 5g

Solve your mid-afternoon sweet cravings with these date boats - they're delicious - and they also come with some nutritious benefits!

Serves 2 Prep Time 4 mins Cook Time 0 mins ## INGREDIENTS 30g (1oz) Stoned Sayer Dates (roughly 8 dates) 12g (1/2oz) Smooth Peanut Butter 1 Square Dark Chocolate (cut into 8 pieces)	## HOW TO COOK IT With a sharp knife, slice the dates down the middle lengthways, ensuring you don't cut through the dates. Measure out the peanut butter and then divide it into 8 pieces (or as many parts to match the number of dates you have). Spoon the peanut butter pieces into the gaps you cut open on each date. It doesn't matter of the peanut butter spills out on top of the dates. Finish off by placing a piece of the dark chocolate on top of the peanut butter. Note: These are great to keep in the fridge for a few days and take to work as a mid-afternoon snack.

DIETICIAN'S NOTES

Dates are nature's dessert - they're super sweet but also deliver fibre and some B vitamins. These date boats are great little energy booster and could be used for a pre-workout fuel top up.

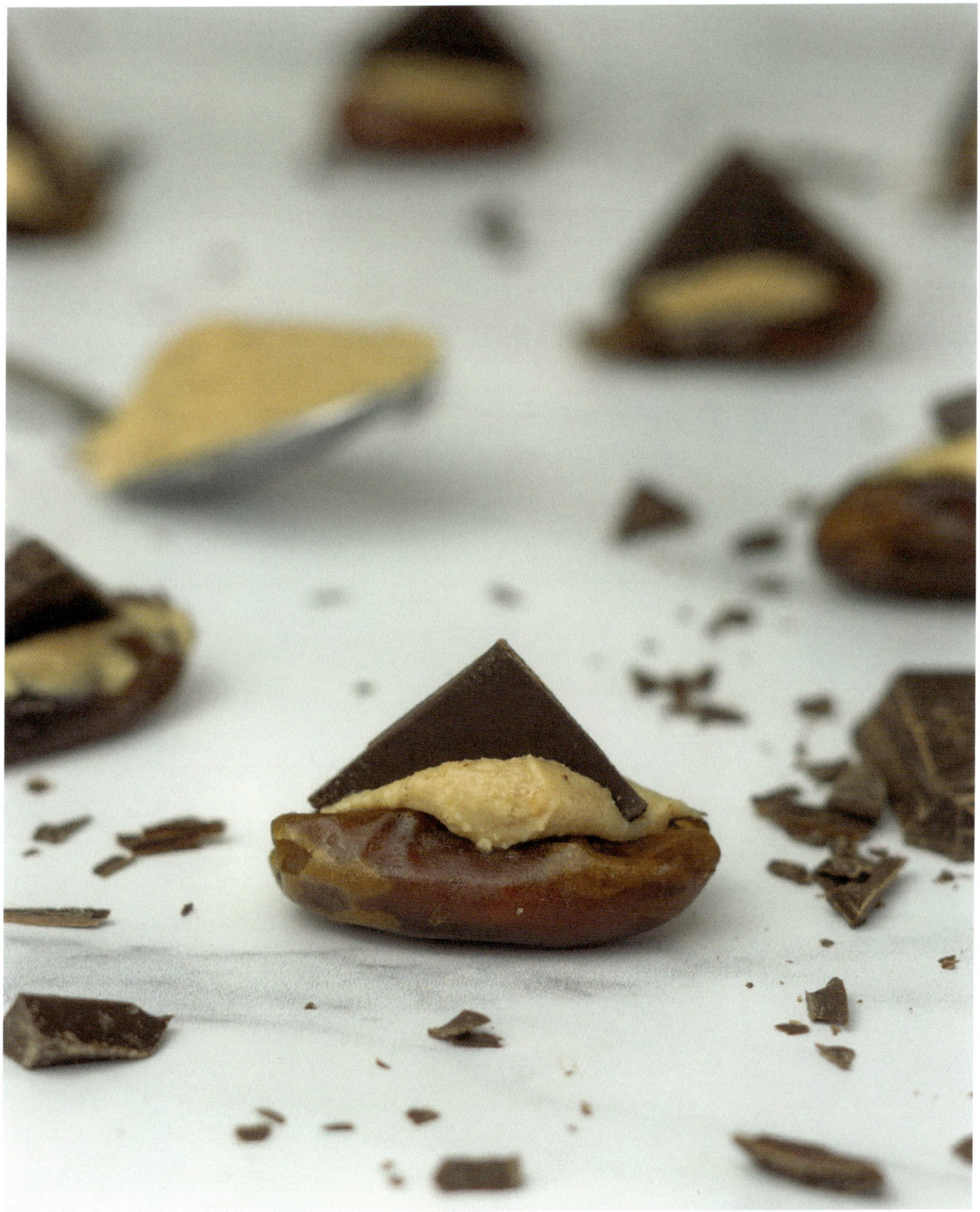

DARK CHOCOLATE & RASPBERRY MUFFINS

(Per Serving) Calories 264 / Carbs 50g / Protein 7g / Fat 4g

These yummy muffins are so easy to make! Fresh raspberries go really well with chocolate, just add bananas, oats and protein powder instead of flour and eggs.

Serves 4 (2 muffins per serving) Prep Time 6 mins Cook Time 22 mins ## INGREDIENTS 120g (4 1/4oz) Rolled Oats 4 Ripe Bananas 1 tbsp Maple Syrup 1 tsp Cinnamon ½ tsp Ground Ginger ½ tsp Nutmeg 1tsp Baking Powder 40g (1 1/2oz) Raspberries 12g (1/2oz) Vegan Chocolate Protein 2 Squares Vegan Dark Chocolate	## HOW TO COOK IT Preheat the oven to 180°C (350°F). Blitz the Oats in the food processor until you have a fine flour. Add the bananas to a large mixing bowl. With a fork, mash them until they become a puree. Add in the remaining ingredients to the banana puree (apart from the dark chocolate). Mix it all together. Tip: Using silicone muffin moulds stops them from sticking. Half fill the muffin moulds with the banana mixture. Then add a raspberry and dark chocolate to each muffin before covering with the remaining mixture. Place in the middle of the oven and cook for 22-24 minutes. Leave to stand for 10 minutes before tucking in.

DIETICIAN'S NOTES

A sweet fix with hidden benefits! The oat flour & bananas are a good source of slow release energy, B vitamins and fibre. These muffins could help fuel a longer endurance workout, or teamed with soya yoghurt and fruits would support post-workout recovery, or just enjoy as a snack

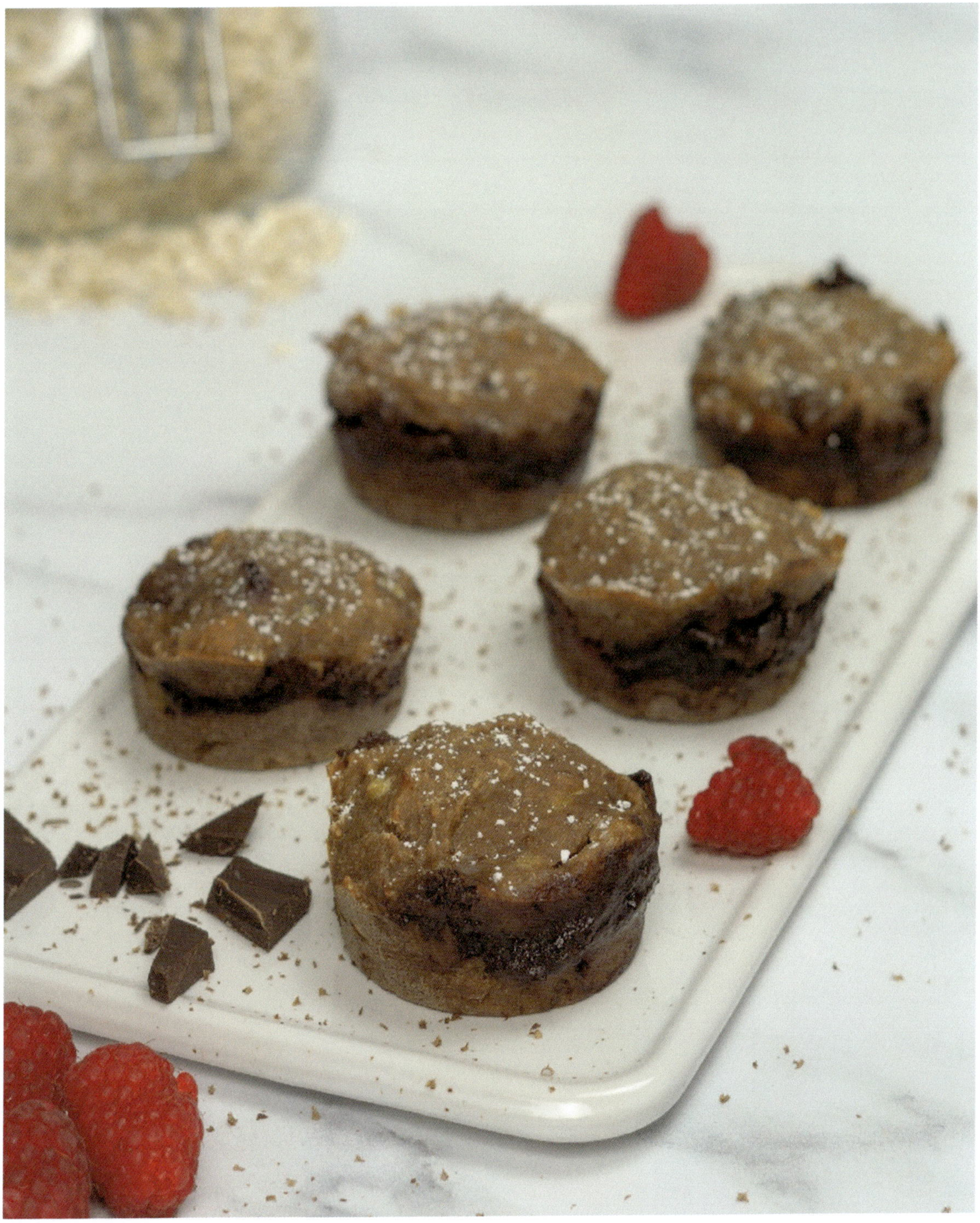

Printed in Great Britain
by Amazon